before Forever

How do you know that you know?

By
Byron and Carla Weathersbee

www.legacyfamily.org
www.beforeforever.com

before**Forever**
copyright©2012 by Byron and Carla Weathersbee
LFM82884wwbtaowd

Weathersbee, Byron and Carla.
　　　Before Forever: How do you know that you know?

ISBN: 978-1-936417-75-9

Cover design by Austin Mann – austinmann.com

Published by PCG Legacy,
a division of Pilot Communications Group, Inc.
Printed in the United States of America

to Bo, Brittney, and Casey
you bring excitement to the legacy journey
…and you keep us authentic

a big thank you to…

…**our parents**, Mac and Carolyn Weathersbee and Barbara Belser (and the late Dr. Bob Belser,) who have passed on a Godly legacy. You have taught us about commitment, love, and faithfulness until death parts…and even after death. We have been blessed to have both sides celebrate their 50th wedding anniversary. What a great legacy you have left.

…**Dave Greene** for being the best writer/editor on the planet earth. The friendship that was developed through this project with Dave and Kathryn will last forever. Thanks Gary Thomas for connecting us…you are still our all time favorite author.

…**Legacy Family Ministries' Board of Directors** who allowed us, and even encouraged us, to pursue this writing project. Darrell and Cindy Janecka, Jay Jeffrey, Kevin and Leslie Rhea, Dr. Kim Scott, and Jeff Walter provided support to implement what has been learned, and helped modify "theory" into real life ministry.

…**all the couples who have shared life with us**. Every couple needs heroes like Frank and Judy Norman, Dr. Randall and Kay O'Brien, Ron and V. Beth Durham, Paul and Jane Meyer, Gary and Donna Dundee, Charlie Baker, Kent and Terri Shirley, Joe and Colleen Palmer, and Phil and Lori Sims. Everyone needs friends in ministry like Terry and Becky Armstrong, Dave and Toni Crowder, Tiger and Leslie Dawson, Ben and Jamie Dudley, Dr. Eddie and Carolyn Helker, Bob and Debbie Johns, David and Cathy Johnson, Jen (and the late Kyle) Lake, Griff and Abby Martin, Jay and Lydia Mathis, Ryan and Kristen Richardson, Dr. Steve Sadler, Dr. Bruce and Susan Wesley, and Chris and Susan Wommack. Every family needs lifelong friends that journey through life right beside you like the Asays, Metcalfs, Millers, Mullins, Powers, Smiths, Ross, and a host of others. These people have all been greatly used by God in the sanctification process of our lives.

...the 1,000+ couples who have been through our *Countdown* marriage preparation course. Since we stumbled into this ministry in 1996, God has greatly used you to shape our lives and ministry. Thanks for taking marriage serious.

...the Baylor baseball teams (1996-2007) for the many discussions at Bible study. All of the discussions had a way of circling back to women and sex. These pages are filled with thoughts that came from your questions, insights, and sick humor.

table of contents

foreword

....

"Mate selection isn't the iTunes store."

This choice quote from the Weathersbees points to *Before Forever*'s importance: who you marry is a complex decision that will likely affect your life more than any other decision you'll ever make, except for the decision to follow Christ. Your marriage will set the climate for your weekdays; it'll heavily influence your weekends; it will color every vacation; it will follow you all the way into old age. Any commitment of such importance cries out for wise discernment—exactly the process that my friends Byron and Carla take you through in this book.

If you start asking the important questions after you've "fallen in love," your ability to objectively answer them will be seriously challenged. The chemical reaction of infatuation is intense and even tyrannical. It is the unusual man or woman who can look past such overwhelming feelings and peer objectively into reality. Infatuation is as overwhelming and affirming as it is blinding and deceitful—which is why you will do well to consider wise counsel before you settle on any one person in particular. That, in short, is another reason why *Before Forever* is so very important.

Making a wise, considered decision about whom you marry can save you much grief and reward you with much joy. Any investment you make in securing a Godly match and choosing a suitable mate will pay off literally every day of your life. You hold in your hands a mighty tool—use it well, and be blessed.

Gary Thomas
Author of *Sacred Marriage*

000 can we trust that inner voice?

....

It was impulsive of me, I know, to go out on a limb and write what I did in that postcard after only two dates with Carla. At the time, however, something inside told me that *she was the one.*

> *But could I trust that little voice inside? If anything, I should have distrusted it, for I'd only recently broken up with my high school sweetheart. So what did that little voice and I really know?*

// Can we trust that voice inside that tells us he or she is the one? //

Carla far exceeded anyone I had imagined would come my way. Spring term had just ended for us at the university we attended when she left to work at a camp for the summer. I can have a pretty one-track mind and so using a blank postcard that a friend of mine had brought back from a recent trip of his to Hawaii, I jotted a note to Carla along with the cryptic note "82884WWBTAOWD" tucked away in the bottom right-hand corner. It looked like a postal code, and no one but me knew that it stood for "We will be there after our wedding day: 8/28/84." Inside I was sure I knew what I wanted, but outside there wasn't a chance I would let anyone know. As much as I was drawn to a life together with Carla, I didn't yet want her to know it!

That was pretty bold of me (or maybe psycho), considering it was three years prior to my projected Hawaiian honeymoon.[1] But I was so smitten by Carla I could have penned the note with my own testosterone. Rereading that postcard today you

---

1 To be honest, I was probably more focused on having passionate sex on a tropical island with my new bride.

can tell that we didn't know each other all that well, but every encounter I'd had with Carla (all two of them!) left me more captivated by this woman.

One of those meetings was at "Rock n' Roll," one of those crazy guy-girl college functions at a skating rink, where the small group Carla was leading and the group of guys that grabbed me decided to gather. Truth be told, I had looked forward to skating in circles about as much as being chained in front of the home decorating channel. But like most hot-blooded college males, at the time I was willing to make an exception if the prospect of picking up a great woman was involved.

As a joke, the DJ played one of those junior high "couples only" songs. It was at that point I realized Carla was *the one*. Not really the one to marry—just the one to ask to skate. My heart was racing as I built up courage to ask Carla. As trite and cheesy as that may sound, my hands sweat more than an evangelist at a summer tent revival when I'm nervous. So for me to ask Carla—whom I didn't really know—to skate with me while holding my sweat-slippery hands took some big-time courage. (Don't laugh. All of us have personal insecurities held over from 7th grade.) I didn't want to gross her out, but I also didn't want to let the opportunity slip by, because in the vernacular of the early 1980's Carla was what my friends and I called a "godly fox."

What a stupid phrase. At the time, however, that saying was "off the hook." Carla had me "crazier than a mug," another phrase with the shelf life of about a month. And though the way we say it changes more often than a university freshman changes majors, the experience down through the centuries remains the same: I soon fully believed Carla was *the one*.[2]

only one? see "entrusted with a great responsibility" | p.176

She was the most beautiful, most Christ-centered, most amazing woman I had ever met. Put bluntly, I was deeply infatuated with her.

Married people often tell singles in that twitter-pated[3] state of mind I was in that spring, "You'll know whether she's the one."

---

2   As if there were only one, "right" person for me to find among the billions out there, like the proverbial needle in a haystack….

3   Oh, come on. Didn't you ever watch the movie *Bambi*? Twitter-pated is that happy, jumpy feeling you get when you are completely enamored with someone. For Bambi (and the other animals) it was the "love" in the air during spring when all the animals lose their minds during mating season.

"But how?" you naturally ask when you begin getting serious.

"Oh, you'll just know."

"But *how*?!" you may think. Often, no one will give you a better answer than "You just *know* that you know," another stupid phrase that needs to go out with 1980's parachute pants.

Yet in spite of all I *didn't* know then, and as presumptuous as my hidden Hawaiian love note was, Carla entered my life somehow as an answer to a question my heart had been asking for years. Something clicked in me when I met her, and I knew that if she was not the girl I would marry, then my future wife would probably be someone an awful lot like her. *That* much I already knew.

If only "knowing that you know" were easier.

But that's precisely the point, we think. Knowing whether she or he is the one isn't easy for a reason. It's difficult because the journey God is leading you on is one that will search *you* to the core. "Knowing that you know" isn't as simple as browsing the Internet to match your online personality profile with some pre-selected mate. Instead it's a journey that will challenge your faith, deepen your trust, and refine who you are in the process.

You see, this journey isn't only about seeking a *yes* or *no* answer to marriage. It's about something much larger, where God's Spirit mysteriously touches our lives and we find God wooing us through our search to "know that we know" into a relationship with Him more beautiful than the very thing you're seeking by picking up this book.

That journey is what this book is all about.

//////////////

introduction
seeking to know

//////////////

001 will you really *just know*?

....

Byron still gives me a hard time about that night at the skating rink, when he really wanted to skate with me and I wanted to include the rest of the gals in my discipleship group sitting off to the side. He had built up the courage to skate with me, he tells me, and before he knew it, he was skating with someone he later said he was not attracted to in the least.[1]

As I watched my friend skate with him, however, I could see in the look on her face that Byron had gone out of his way to make her feel special nevertheless. *He certainly is cute*, I thought as I watched him skate round the rink, but it was the way he treated my friend that deepened my respect for him. He stood apart from all the other guys I knew who were preoccupied with getting into the right fraternity and speaking their lingo. I found myself intrigued by Byron that evening and thinking about what it would be like to spend more time with him.

// Will I really "just know"? //

But although the initial attraction was there between us, did I really believe early on that we might marry? Though I was attracted to him, marriage was one of the furthest things from my mind.

On some level, everyone assesses their compatibility and chemistry—or they should—as they first get to know the other person in a serious relationship headed toward marriage. You either think, *I can see myself connecting with this person for years to come*, or, *This person bugs me*.

....

1   "A short, 'heavy-set' girl with a great personality" was how he put it. Name withheld to protect the innocent.

As I got to know Byron over the months that followed, the more everything about us seemed to match. But we were also young and naïve, both flying high on enthusiasm and probably overly confident about that next phase of our lives and relationship. After several months, we thought we were *so* compatible, *so* ready to marry.

All of us begin running down a mental list that we've developed throughout life, checking off the areas we feel the other person matches up: *Does he know where he's going in life? Am I attracted to her? Is he sensitive and affectionate? Is she confident? Do we enjoy some of the same interests? How does she relate to God? Is God calling us in a similar direction?* It's a list most of us develop subconsciously and, consequently, often assess subconsciously.

does my partner match my list? | p.099

You may have even written a list that might look something like this:

- Great looking, good sense of humor
- Godly Christian who has a daily quiet time...even journals daily
- Pure—a virgin or maybe someone who kissed dating goodbye
- Never gets angry
- Rugged masculine tough guy who knows how to express his feelings. Or a soft, beautiful graceful, feminine "hotty" that drives a jeep and jumps out of airplanes for thrills.
- No character flaws
- Parents not divorced

Unfortunately, not even Jesus Christ would pass some of our lists.

But the problem with tying our decision too closely to our mental lists is that…well, we're the one who created them. And how is it possible to be objective about the most subjective subject in the world—our very own self? Are we humble enough to admit that we might not actually know what we need?

Are our mental lists enough to go by?

Intuition: Telltale Clue or Jumping to Conclusions?

Back to that cryptic postcard from Hawaii I sent Carla. Did I really have the intuition to know I was going to marry Carla? Or did I embrace a "believe it and achieve it" mindset?

//   What am I to make of my intuition?   //

First, it is important for you to know (but don't let Carla know) that this was not the first time I had this "intuition." You know how guys sometimes see a good-looking girl from a distance and say, "I am going to marry that woman!" We have a friend named Will, who was overheard on several occasions telling hot girls that "he was God's *Will* for her life."[2]

So what do we do with those "Hawaii postcard moments"?

Well, it is important to understand that

intuition is simply

our reason working on a subconscious level.

Intuition can provide clues to what we feel deep inside, but those clues *may or may not be trusted.*

There's a story about physiologist Otto Loewi, who awoke one night in the early morning hours, having dreamt of a chemistry experiment that would help him solve a problem in his study of human nerves. He got up, jotted down some notes, and then went back to sleep. The next morning, however, he found he could not decipher his own writing. Thankfully, his subconscious mind was still at work and the next night he had the same dream. This time, upon waking, he went at once to work in his laboratory, and the results of his experiment led him to receive the Nobel Prize for Medicine.

---

2   Can you feel your gag reflex kick in?

That, my friend, is why in college I used to sleep with my textbooks under my pillow, just hoping that osmosis or something subconscious would take place to get me out of studying. Because you have to admit that it's pretty amazing what our minds are capable of accomplishing in the background. But as remarkable as that story is, Loewi's dreamed-up experiment doesn't come close to comparing to the complexity of intuiting who to marry.

As your relationship develops and marriage begins to feel less like something you dream of doing and more of something you might actually do, the question, *how do I* really *know if we should marry?* takes on greater significance. It becomes *the* question needing an answer, yet many people still rely on intuition by responding, "Oh, you'll just know," as if the answer came as easily as breathing. But if you, too, give in to the superficial idea that you'll "just know" without going any further, you cut yourself off from the very journey God will likely use to take you to a place of deeper understanding regarding yourself and your relationship's future.

Unfortunately, intuition is often untrustworthy because we can be attracted to someone not only because of healthy hopes, but also because of our unrealistic dreams and past hurts needing attention. Sometimes our intuition provides just the telltale clue we need to find our way; at other times it leads us far astray. The fact is, most of us don't "just know," and at times are left with more questions than answers:

are our parents for or against it?... | p.187

- *Are we really compatible? Are our families compatible?*
- *What does it look like practically "to have and to hold from this day forward"?*
- *How can I truly know whether or not I should marry him or her when I'm making the decision from a biased perspective?!*

do I have my "stuff" together? | p.195

Certainly you want to marry someone who shares similar values, direction, and interests. But addressing the question of *whom* to marry assumes that you are *ready* to marry and that you know what marriage is about—its nature and demands. Consequently, instead of asking, *How will I know whom to marry?* or *Is this the one?*, a better starting point is to ask yourself such questions as *Do I know who I am?*, *Am I ready for marriage?*, and *If I'm to enter into this relationship that is 'till death do us part,'* *what is God's intent for that relationship?* Many people talk about marriage as if it is a foregone conclusion, but all of us must first assess whether or not we are even ready to marry.

Did Byron and I need to continue to seek God's wisdom in prayer? Sure. God encourages us to ask Him for help, especially when our experience doesn't measure up to the decisions before us: *"If any of you lacks wisdom, he should ask God, who gives generously to all without finding fault, and it will be given to him"* (James 1:5). Was it wise to get to know one another over a period of time to assess that the blend and balance between us was a good one? Of course.

We both still needed time for God to confirm what He was doing in each of our lives by bringing us together—time to allow the chaotic cloud of infatuation to dissipate and expose what *true* beauty really lay at the heart of our relationship.

"Beauty" > Chaos > Real Beauty

I (Carla) never really saw Byron lose his temper until our relationship was quite serious. One Saturday after a hectic week, we headed off to a wedding about three hours away. We left late, got lost (in my opinion, not Byron's),[3] and then got stuck behind a logging truck on a two-lane road. At that point Byron realized he had taken a wrong turn (although he was never "officially" lost) and we were 45 minutes away from a wedding scheduled to begin in 25 minutes.

He *lost* it!

He yelled, beat his fist into the steering wheel, and hit the dash repeatedly. Talk about uncomfortable. It was as if everything was out of control...especially Byron. I had never seen that side of him.

My knight in shinning armor had turned into an idiot in a metal suit.

....
3   Byron wants everyone to know he was never lost. It was a "short cut gone bad."

Most of us think of *chaos* as complete disorder: getting lost on the way to a friend's wedding, the violent surprise of being broadsided at a four-way intersection; the helpless, inevitable decay into death of a loved one; the sinking feeling at 2 a.m. when your computer's hard drive explodes into digital shrapnel the night before a final term paper is due. All of these, many of us think, describe chaos. But while chaos *can* mean that at its extremes, the concept is much more complex and rich.

At the beginning of most any relationship possibly leading to marriage, no one but your partner seems more perfect, and no one may be able to convince you otherwise. *Infatuation*, we call it. It's that feeling in which *everything* seems to make sense on the surface—because the surface is all that you've seen. It's an exciting time filled with what feels like ironclad optimism, but infatuation is simply one initial phase in a relationship. It's a two-dimensional look at a person, air-brushed and given "depth" by our own imaginations that fill in the gaps, coloring our partner as brilliant, the perfectly loyal friend, and the consummate lover. It's our nature to hope for the best when it comes to marriage, so who doesn't feel at least a touch of infatuation at first?

But when reality begins to seep in you begin to see the contradictions, the irksome behaviors, the hot temper, and the blatant sinfulness in that other person's life—and in your *own* life. These complexities begin to pile atop one another like a collapsing house of cards, and soon that seriously dating relationship may feel like complete disorder of your mind, emotions, social life—even physical and spiritual aspects of who you are.

What is happening?, you may find yourself asking. It may feel like your relationship is falling apart—but it may be your shallow *idea* of the relationship that is falling apart, while a much deeper, more lasting relationship is being built. You are probably simply seeing things for the way they truly are.

Webster's New Millennium Dictionary of English defines chaos theory, which deals with these complexities, as "the study of unpredictable and complex dynamic systems that are highly sensitive to small changes in external conditions." Think of it this way: chaos is an intensely complex system such as our weather, our economy, or, better yet, any intimate relationship—especially a serious relationship possibly leading to marriage. *Chaos*, which is based on an ancient Greek word meaning "gaping void," is about too many variables all mingling together for us to predict the precise outcome, let alone identify all of the contributing factors.

You may have heard of the "butterfly effect," which says that the smallest disturbance from just one butterfly flapping its wings can create a chain reaction of events like falling dominoes, with the potential to eventually create a hurricane on the other side of the world. In essence, that single flap of a butterfly's wing can be one of those many parts of a weather's system that leads to something much greater. More often than not, however, a butterfly will flap its wings and create only the slightest disturbance in the air that leads to nothing. Chaos, then, is the unknown everything that can happen between nothing and the hurricane.

The possibilities kind of blow your mind, don't they?[4] And when it comes to making a decision of whether or not to marry, that mind-blowing reality is part of the problem. Every person's relationship initially feels simple, uncomplicated, and euphoric before the complexity and chaotic confusion sets in.

But as intimidating as that chaotic void may be, growing exponentially in its complexity as you move closer together, chaos also serves as the blank canvas on which creation occurs. God uses that very chaos that *feels* so disorienting as a means to orient us, to better understand ourselves and our relationship, if we are attentive.

From the beginning of humanity in the book of Genesis we see this lived out.

> *God created the Heavens and Earth—all you see, all you don't see.*
> *Earth was a soup of nothingness, a bottomless emptiness, and inky*

----

4   It's like one of those sci-fi movies in which multiple universes begin to open, each with unique visions of the way life could be.

blackness…. God spoke: "Let us make human beings in our image
make them reflecting our nature. So they can be responsible for…
Earth itself, and every animal that moves on the face of Earth."[5]

Only the Creator of the Universe can take chaos—the unknown, infinite possibilities—and shape them into something beautiful, His beauty.

There is no way for us to know for sure what path your relationship will take, for there are simply too many possibilities. As Mike Mason writes in his book *The Mystery of Marriage*, "…a person is the single most limitless entity in creation, and if there is anything that is even more unlimited and unrestrained in its possibilities than is a person, then it is two people together."[6] And because there are an infinite number of paths our lives (and, consequently, serious dating relationships) could take, *every* couple's story is different.

Which path will your relationship take? There are no easy answers to that question. But again, that is precisely the point. That is the journey of discovery you are traveling, and the uncertainty you may feel is all part of it.

Even if along the way you are "late" for the wedding.[7]

---

5   Genesis 1:1-2, 26 (*The Message*)

6   Mason, Mike. *The Mystery of Marriage*. (Sisters: Multnomah Press, 1985): 14.

7   We arrived at the wedding just in time to see the father present the bride to be married.

002 what is God *doing*?

....

When asked to explain his theory of general relativity, Albert Einstein once jokingly responded, "Put your hand on a hot stove for a minute, and it seems like an hour. Sit with a pretty girl for an hour, and it seems like a minute. That's relativity!"[1]

I could certainly relate to that when I was with Carla, who made hours seem like minutes.

[Driving question: Is there some kind of formula to help make the decision?]

Einstein's famous formula behind general relativity, $e=mc^2$, changed our understanding of the universe and has helped explain such mind-bending ideas as how mass and energy are equivalent, how matter warps the "fabric" of space, and how moving at the speed of light contracts time.

Although my man Albert was brilliant, I am almost certain that he was unable to figure out in his lab how to find a woman. (Have you seen pictures of this man? I'm not sure how he ever found a woman.) Who knows, maybe he used an equation he never wanted to share with the rest of us because his first marriage ended after sixteen years…and then he married his cousin that same year.[2]

Einstein's physics blows our minds, but scientists are still in search of what they call the "grand, unified theory," which bridges quantum mechanics and general relativity—one single equation able to describe every physical phenomena in the universe, from physics to biology to chemistry, from the movement of molecules to

1   http://www.anecdotage.com/index.php?aid=14050 , quoting *New Chronicle*, March 14, 1949.
2   *Nobel Lectures, Physics 1901-1921* (Amsterdam: Elsevier Publishing Company, 1967).

the movement of galaxies. That theory—when it is finally discovered—will speak volumes about the simple, elegant beauty with which God created His universe.

Unfortunately, when it comes to knowing whether or not you should marry that person who makes hours seem like minutes, as important as wisdom and counsel are to deciding who to marry, and as insightful as compatibility tests may be—mate selection[3] cannot also be reduced to one simple formula.

It just can't.

Try to come up with a formula to predict successful mate selection[4] and you will come up with some very helpful principles (which we'll discuss in the chapters to come), but, ultimately, the contributing factors simply become too many to predict marital success with absolute accuracy. With so many variables at work, it takes something far beyond our natural human ability to guide the process.

Something supernatural.

God Only Knows.

While in search of the right answer, it might be more important to acknowledge the overall process. In the classes I teach at Baylor, it drives me crazy when a student raises a hand and asks, "Hey, Dr. B, is this going to be on the exam?" In my opinion, professors should never teach content merely for the sake of an exam question.

Good professors teach *students—not content*.

// Is there a common denominator for successful relationships? //

I love the story of William Phelps, an American scholar and Yale professor of English literature in the early 1900's. He was once grading exams shortly before Christmas

---

3 Man, we need a new term. Can somebody help us?
4 There is that word again…

when he came across one student's answer to one of his more difficult test questions: "God only knows the answer to this question. Merry Christmas."

Phelps wrote the following comment on the paper: "God gets an *A*, you get an *F*—Happy New Year!" [5]

When it comes to knowing "beyond a shadow of a doubt" whether your relationship will be a lasting match, quite literally God only knows the answer. That's both the risk and the adventure of marriage—of *any* close relationship really. That isn't to say that in our decision making we should become "so heavenly minded that we are of no earthly good," becoming hyper-spiritual and grasping for some mystical, out-of-the-clouds answer to the question of whom to marry. God doesn't want us to ignore the obvious in front of our noses in order to receive some disembodied answer. In other words, when we look to God for an answer it doesn't mean letting go of our God-given senses.

Of course, trusting the wise counsel of His Spirit in us is invaluable to our success. If God can be trusted with creating the universe—making something from nothing—surely He can be trusted with making something out of our lives. Indeed, He is the only one who can bring true, deep, three-dimensional beauty out of the chaos and two-dimensional infatuation.

Over the years of working with engaged and pre-engaged couples, we have listened to literally hundreds of stories of how people met and ultimately ended up at the altar—or didn't. While some of these stories resemble each other somewhat, most are as unique as a person's fingerprints. But in every case, whether a seriously dating couple marries or not, one common denominator is that God is present every step of the way, always working to help re-create us into the people He intends us to be, always pointing the way for us to "become mature, attaining to the whole measure of the fullness of Christ" (Eph. 4:13b), whoever we may be.

Chances are, the details of how you and your partner met and how your relationship has developed don't resemble others' stories. Your personality,

---

5   http://www.anecdotage.com/index.php?aid=3545 , quoting E. Fuller, *2500 Anecdotes; Daily Telegraph*, July 22, 1987.

maturity, life circumstances and timing, family background, and past experiences in relationships—not to mention chemistry and compatibility with your partner—all mingle to create unique paths as you consider whether or not to marry. For some, the decision begins with starry, high hopes and dreams (perhaps too high); for others, the decision leads through the hard reality of pain as they recall broken relationships in their past. Some need time to be reassured that their marriage won't look a thing like their parents' marriage; others want nothing more in life than a beautiful marriage like the one their parents had. Outside forces—such as college graduation, military service, or a job opportunity in another state—may shorten or lengthen your path…or cut it off altogether. In short, who you are apart from your mate and who you are in relationship to God will influence who you are together and what your path will look like as you come together—so no one's path will look like yours.

It would be easy to assume that those relationships that look picture perfect are guaranteed success. But in our years of working with pre-engaged and engaged couples, we have also seen relationships where we thought, *now* they *are Ken and Barbie; what a great couple*—and they've struggled in their marriage because while their relationship *appeared* successful, that kind of beauty is only skin deep. On occasion, a few of those relationships have ended in divorce. On the other hand, we have also seen relationships where we thought, *get a clue, you guys should* not *get married*—and they're doing great. They have wonderful marriages, they're serving faithfully in their community, and life is going well.

Why do some relationships appear ideal, only to succumb to relational disintegration or divorce, while other couples' relationships seem to be a train wreck waiting to happen, only to develop into faithful, deeply committed marriages years later?

What makes the difference?

Wrestling to Know that You Know.

It may seem strange, but some who marry certainly aren't ready, yet as they submit their lives to God, He works in miraculous ways to bring them through the difficult times and help them learn to better love one another. Other couples' marriages, which from all outside appearances seem straight out of a fairy tale, expose hearts in need of deep transformation. If those hearts don't change, that couple may be in danger of divorcing. People marry for all sorts of unhealthy reasons:

as a desperate cure for loneliness,

as an escape from parents or an act of revenge against them,

as an addict's fix for lust,

for financial security,

because of cultural expectations,

and the list goes on and on.

While God, of course, is always at work in our lives, we often work at cross purposes with Him.

//   God is always at work in our relationships—sure—but how?   //

We'll spend some time assessing your motivations for marriage in the coming chapters to make sure that you are working in concert with God, because certainly much of what makes the difference between a healthy relationship and an unhealthy relationship is God's presence in our lives and growing in His ways of sacrificial love.

why do I do what I do? | p.075

why am I in this relationship? | p.083

Should it surprise us that God is always behind the scenes, endeavoring to work good for each person in every situation? For God knows each one of our stories, our past, our hopes and dreams. Isn't that in keeping with His gracious, persistent effort? He knows each of our strengths and weaknesses, and has already been helping each one of us write the story of our lives. God's knowledge of who we are and what we need goes infinitely beyond our own—and He has the ability to bring *true* beauty out of the chaos of two complex individuals moving together in an even more complex relationship.

Looking to God for an answer of whether or not you should marry isn't a one-time event, like having your name called over the intercom when your table is ready at a restaurant. Much more likely than hearing a voice from above, God will lead you on a journey of discovery. While you may be seeking a stamp of validation on your relationship, He may likely hold back on a simple thumbs-up or thumbs-down, guiding you instead along a seemingly indirect path as you seek what He is doing in your life. So as you and your partner read through this book, hold your relationship loosely before you hold it tightly in a marital covenant. Talk with God about your hopes, doubts, and fears; let His ways permeate yours and His Spirit inform your actions. God has given us great freedom and all sorts of resources to make this decision of whether or not to become engaged:

- Reason to help us cut through the confusing emotions.
- Emotions to help us feel the full range of human experience in the relationship.
- Intuition to warn us when our emotions or other factors may be leading us astray.
- Wise counsel from those with more life experience to give us a healthy, outside perspective.

But while God has given us these abilities and resources, they are never meant to substitute for walking through the decision with God yourself, looking to Him as an intimate friend at your side listening to and considering your innermost thoughts as you share them.

It takes deep, honest soul-searching to reach below the surface. I remember one couple who went though our marriage prep program after dating throughout college. Their relationship seemed right, friends and family agreed on the match—in fact, nothing about them during our marriage prep class sent up a red flag. But less than a year into the marriage, she announced that she had been living a lie and just could not believe in a God she could not see. She had played the game well, but her relationship with God was a facade. God, of course, saw to the heart of this "perfect couple," but on the surface she fooled everyone—her friends, her husband...and herself.

Knowledge of Knowing.

//   What kind of knowledge is needed to help us "know that we know"?   //

Knowing *about* your relationship from a limited human perspective—what activities the two of you enjoy together, how your personalities complement each other, and what direction you're both headed in life—as important as that is, is not ultimately what will cause a relationship to succeed or not, for our relationships with one another were intended from the beginning of time to be lived out within the context of a relationship with a Holy God. Sure, your knowledge, by the grace of God, may point you in the right direction, but it won't keep you going when all the strength you can muster to love is depleted. Scripture says, "Fear of the LORD is the beginning of knowledge" (Proverbs 1:7), and it is a holy relationship with God that screws our heads on straight as we prepare to enter marriage. When we fear God and His holy ways and begin to be formed by His presence in our lives, we begin to know what to do, how to respond—even what to decide—because we have a holy fear of the Lord and His ways. The book of Proverbs puts it like this:

> [5] *Trust GOD from the bottom of your heart;*
>   *don't try to figure out everything on your own.*
> [6] *Listen for GOD'S voice in everything you do, everywhere you go;*
>   *he's the one who will keep you on track.*
> [7] *Don't assume that you know it all.*
>   *Run to GOD! Run from evil!*
> *(Proverbs 3:5-7 The Message)*

Many people talk *about* God and offer "wise, Godly" principles—yet they may overlook encouraging you to respond in trust to the very One who is the source of all wisdom. For years couples we knew who honeymooned in Maui told us about taking a jeep along the stunning, shoreline road to Hana, riding bikes down the volcano Haleakala, and seeing the most luminous double rainbows known to man. But until Byron and I experienced Maui firsthand on our 20th anniversary, it was only secondhand. Let me just tell you there is a big difference in seeing someone else's photos and getting to experience Maui.

The same is true with God's wisdom.

You see, exercising "wisdom" apart from God is no wisdom at all. In fact, Scripture says that this is a defining mark of a *fool*, one who is "wise in his own eyes."[6] Only when God is primary in your life do the secondary principles follow:

- Assessing the ways you balance each other and together form a cohesive unit
  what do I bring to the table? | p.063
- Recognizing your false expectations and the realities of what it means to be married
  does my partner match my list? | p.099
- Setting emotional and physical boundaries
  do I guard my heart or give my heart away? | p.123
  what do i do with this sex-driven life? | p.131
- Considering the different ways we give and receive love
  "I love you" no strings attached? | p.141
- Sizing up the sacrifice and commitment necessary for a marriage
  why is commitment so difficult...? | p.155
- Praying toward a future together
  from commitment to covenant? | p.173

No matter how well the two of you score on relationship compatibility tests, if God's sacrificial love is not evident and growing in your lives, then giving yourself selflessly in marriage will always be a difficult task. I (Byron) don't know about you, but for me to drum up enough love for Carla that is patient, kind, gentle, self-controlled, and not self-seeking *apart* from God is impossible. Heaven knows how many times I've tried being gentle simply because that's the role of a loving husband—but that wears off pretty quickly. In fact, I could probably tell you a hundred stories in which I tried to jump through the hoops of being loving in and of myself to impress Carla. But let me give you just one.

---

6   Proverbs 12:15, 26:5, 26:12, 28:11

Throughout our two years of dating (and well into marriage for that matter), I demonstrated my "self-controlled" disciplined life by jogging with Carla. She loves to run, loves everything about it—especially the euphoric feeling after a hard workout.

I hate to run, however. I hate the feeling before, during, and after a run. Nothing about running is fun for me. Running is punishment. Running is something you're made to do on 95-degree August afternoons when you throw a bad pass or cuss at football practice.

For a few years, I was able to bluff my way into Carla's heart as a disciplined athlete who cared about my body. But just like that couple who looked great on the outside, I can only play *that* game for a short time. Truth be known, I struggle with self-control. And when it came to running, I had "coach-discipline," not "self-discipline." So when I got tired of impressing Carla, I quit. I quit running. I quit everything and sat my fat butt on the couch in an attempt to hit 200 pounds by the year 2000. (Not a bad slogan, huh: "*200 by 2000!*")

In 1987, at 170 pounds, I still had a long way to go.

But over the last twenty years, God has taught me a lot about myself. He's gently pointed out that not being in control of my physical body is a weakness of mine. The good news is that even at my weakest points, where I'm most incapable, I have a Savior to whom I can yield those parts of my life. Fortunately for me, one of the fruits of the Spirit is "self-control." Put another way, when I know the Spirit of God is working in my life, I see evidence of control in the little things like eating and working out and how I spend my time.[7] God is at work both in the simple and complex parts of my being.

So while working out may be of limited gain, as the apostle Paul says,[8] God is at work even there.

....

7   But I still hate to run!
8   1 Timothy 4:8

Don't Shortcut the Process.

> //   Are you trying to shortcut the process by jumping to a yes-no answer
> regarding whether or not to get engaged?   //

Here's the deal. If you find yourself reading this book solely to extract its principles as a way to answer the question, *should we get married?*, you will miss one of the book's main points: that behind the next step in your relationship—whatever that step may be—is a God who knows you better than you know yourself, who loves you more deeply than you will ever love or be humanly loved, and who wants the best for you and His kingdom. As important as that question is of whether or not you should marry, if all you seek as you go through this book is a *yes* or *no* answer, "you may get what you want," as the saying goes, "but if you leave God out of the mix, you may not like what you get."

We may bring all our psychological wisdom, personality tests, wise counsel, and compatibility exercises to bear on our decision—yet, at the heart, what matters most is being submitted to God, His loving ways, and His intent for our lives before we ever make that choice. You and your partner may be as compatible as they come, but if you're not set on the inside to give sacrificially, to grow in grace, and to lay down your life for the other person, then you will always be striving against one another.

As you consider the principles within this book, talk through issues together as a couple and don't seek a quick answer to your question of whether or not the two of you are ready to marry. Wrestle with the complexities that make up your relationship and earnestly seek God as you do, for these are part of the journey that God will use to bring you to your decision. You may bump up against uncertainties, but remember that they are all part of the process of discovery that God is leading you through.

As we embark on this journey together, allow yourself to explore these questions: *What is God doing in my life now through my relationship? What is He calling me to?*

What is the reference point by which I make my decisions, and what are the values that shape my life?

It will make all the difference as the two of you go through the hard, inner work of arriving at a place in which you both know that you know.

....

When Rowdy and Anna met at a Young Life camp, fireworks were ignited.

Anna was the most amazing girl Rowdy had ever met, and Anna was caught up by Rowdy's aggressive sense of humor. He captivated the Young Life staff—not an easy task with so many funny people gathered in one place. As they worked together on kitchen work crew over the summer their hearts began to be drawn to each other. Long conversations while washing dishes led to one of those Hollywood-scripted moments together on the beach. You know the scene. As the sun set, they began to drop their guard in free-flowing conversation and found they had the same vision and passion for Christ. They laughed; they shared; they entered each other's worlds, matching dreams and lifestyle plans. And they both liked what they saw. It was at that moment that Rowdy just knew that this was the one!

He knew that he knew. After all, you just *know*. Right?

Rowdy transferred to Anna's university so that they could see each other in all seasons of life. They sacrificed and grew as they experienced the *up's* and *down's* of dating seriously. Finally, after a few break-up and make-up experiences, Rowdy and Anna decided to get married.

But then Rowdy made a tactical error. He asked Anna to marry him without first asking her father. The conversation went something like this:

"Will you marry me?"

"Oh, my gosh. Have you asked my dad?"

Which wasn't exactly the response he'd expected.

"No, but your dad and mom can be the first ones we call."

"But you don't understand. This is *really* important to my dad. We've talked about this, Rowdy. My dad *needs* to give his blessing."

"I'm sure he won't mind. Trust me, go call your dad."

Well, Dad was *not* happy, which made for rocky days ahead. Deep down, Dad had never felt good about this relationship, but he was appalled that Rowdy would ask his daughter to marry him without first seeking his blessing. What might seem like a small matter of preference began to uncover are our parents for or against it?... | p.187 deeper issues: the fact that Rowdy plowed through life like an ice-breaker through frozen seas and that Anna was content to follow in his wake. If Rowdy ever found himself in trouble, he used his charm and humor to wiggle out of it. Anna's parents, however, saw right through him. Rowdy was a bright, sharp-tongued, make-it-happen kind of guy who lived life in the fast lane. While Anna loved those traits, her parents also saw that Rowdy could be controlling, unkind, and sometimes verbally abusive. Then, when the couple went through our marriage prep course, the financial section threw them for a loop: Rowdy was in huge debt due to "bad investments," as he put it. (You and I might call it gambling on sports.) This and other things began to shake Anna's does my partner match my list? | p.099 confidence. *Still*, both of them thought, *if we could just get married, share life, and regain focus on our vision that we talked about that evening at Young Life camp, then some of those issues would resolve themselves—wouldn't they?*

So Anna moved to New York where Rowdy was working to be in the same city and regain their ministry and lifestyle vision. But New York agreed with Midwestern-raised Anna as well as bad take-out food. Although in her mind Anna desired to serve and love God with reckless abandon, she wondered whether it really needed to involve all that noise; all those dirty, unkempt people; expensive rent for a nasty one-room apartment; and that hectic subway-chasing, taxi-hailing, look-no-one-in-the-eyes lifestyle. She had grown up in the suburbs of a Midwestern city, where the greatest dangers included staying out of the path of families out for an evening bike ride together in the park. Over time, Anna began to accept who she was and find security in the fact that she did not have to live Rowdy's recklessly abandoned life in order to be obedient to what God desired for her.

In fact, the more time they spent together—as their intimacy began to reveal each person's complexity in all their wonderful, unique facets—the more it seemed that the relationship was not working.

"When we input all the data," Rowdy said, "we got 'syntax error.'"

Digging for Truth Beneath the "Why's?"

//   What do I do with these questions I have,
these seeming "syntax errors" in our relationship?
How do life and our relationship reveal God's Truth?   //

When a "syntax error" pops up—when your relationship that once clicked now clunks—it forces you to search more deeply for the truth about yourself and your partner. You may feel turned inside out by the questions running through your mind: *Why don't things seem to be going as well as they used to? Or, if we're such a great fit, then why do I still feel unsettled about taking the next step into marriage?*

But think about it. Truth lies beneath those *why's*. Some of our most important life lessons we learn by asking these soul-searching questions.

As curious children, we all came to learn that there is more to life than meets the eye. When our son, Bo, was two years old, he asked, "Why is the sky blue?" We would respond, "God made it that way?"

"Why did God make it that way?"

"Well, He just did."

"But *whhhyyy*?"

Even a two-year-old somehow knows there are greater reasons behind *why* the sky is the color blue. And so he kept on asking, *why?* Somehow he knew instinctively that there are layers upon layers of truth that go all the way down to something much larger than himself.

What was true then for Bo is true now for you. Not only is there layer upon layer of truth in answer to our questions, but drill down and you ultimately arrive at Truth with a capital *T*, an encounter with God Himself. Through our human relationships we're continually confronted by the image of God—His character reflected in the lives of those around us—in the consequences we face and the responses of others when we love or hurt them, imperfect though they are. Which is to say that the very questions our relationships raise ultimately point us back to God's work in our life if we dig deeply enough.

I (Carla) love learning about the human body. It fascinates me. But it isn't just reading about the inner workings of the body that I enjoy or sitting in anatomy class and talking for hours about the heart. All that is important, but in the lab the concepts and theories and lectures and book learning and illustrations *come alive* as we dig even more deeply. We can talk about the efficiency of the human body, but in the lab I understand at a more foundational level how red blood cells pass through the chambers of the heart, partnering with the lungs to become oxygenated in order to supply the body with energy. As we begin to better understand the mysteries that confront us, more questions lead to new hypotheses. Years of questioning and trial-and-error in the lab provide valuable information that we can then apply to improve our quality of life. "Knowing is not enough," the German writer Goethe said. "We must apply!"

This practical application makes knowledge powerful.

The same is true in life. Our questions about our relationship lead to more questions (which often lead to…well, more questions), which eventually lead to greater understanding, which leads to knowledge—or, in this case, wisdom. "Science is organized knowledge," Immanuel Kant said. "Wisdom is organized life."

We may have an idea how relationships work, but until we actually have a relationship, we won't know in the same way what makes them succeed or fail, or what love is and isn't. We can talk about love and read about it in Scripture, but until we actually begin the trial-and-error lab work of growing close to someone in a relationship, questioning the weaknesses our relationship reveals, probing for answers, and applying what we learn, we're not going to grow in wisdom, which helps us "know that we know."

If we don't drill down deep with our soul-searching questions and then act on the answers we find, we will begin going through the motions in our relationships.

Doing and saying things for superficial reasons.

Wandering aimlessly.

Wandering in the Land of Nod.

Once, long ago, two brothers each brought God a sacrifice, something from the fruit of their work to honor Him as their provider. The older brother, a farmer named Cain, brought some of his produce from the fields, while the younger brother, a cattle rancher named Abel, brought some meat from the animals in his herd. God loved the younger brother's meat, but the older brother's veggies didn't go over well at all. As with most siblings, when little brother shows up big brother, there is trouble.

In this case, *big* trouble.

God asked Cain,

Why are you angry? Why is your face downcast? If you do what is right, will you not be accepted? But if you do not do what is right, sin is crouching at the door; it desires to have you, but you must master it.[1]

Cain didn't respond to God's second chance to "do what is right," nor to His warnings of what would happen if he didn't. In fact, the whole situation ticked off Cain. And rather than taking charge over the anger inside, Cain was mastered by it and took his little brother out into the field and killed him. God confronted Cain, who talked smack back to God (and you really shouldn't do this). So God cursed Cain by driving him out of the land and causing him to become a homeless wanderer. The story gets worse for Cain, for it reads, "Cain went out from the LORD's presence and lived in the land of Nod, east of Eden."[2]

He *left the presence of God* and wandered in No Man's Land.

Ouch.

All this over bringing vegetables instead of meat?! How can we *not* return to that question we've been asking since childhood:

Why?!

Why was Abel's sacrifice "better" in God's eyes?

Is God simply a meat-and-potatoes kind of God?

Did Cain miss the memo on bringing meat?

What is the Truth beneath what appears to be a bad case of God playing favorites?

---

1 Genesis 4:6-7.
2 Genesis 4:16. (See Genesis 4:1-16 for the story)

Seriously, does Cain's punishment match his crime? In other words, *what in the world is God doing?!*

The Thought that *Really* Counts.

// What does God yearn for in His relationship with us? //

Have you ever heard someone say after they've received a gift, "It's the thought that counts"? What did that person mean by that? Did he mean, "I didn't get what I wanted, but that's okay"? Was he disappointed by not getting what he wanted, or did he mean something else by it?

With God, it isn't so much the gift that matters. It's the giver that really counts; for God, the *giver* is the gift. You see, God doesn't need vegetables or meat. He doesn't even really need our time or money or any other of our *things*, per se. What He wants is your *heart*. He yearns for your life to be close to His, for your heart to beat in sync with His. Later in the Bible, the writer of Hebrews draws our attention back to these two brothers and gives us some insight into what happened with each of their hearts:

> By an act of faith, Abel brought a better sacrifice to God than Cain. It was what he believed, not what he brought, that made the difference. That's what God noticed and approved as righteous. After all these centuries, that belief continues to catch our notice.[3]

Did *you* catch that?

It was Abel's beliefs behind his action that made all the difference. So while he brought choice cuts of meat—the very best he had—it wasn't the meat God was pleased with.

It was his *heart* that made the *thing* valuable.

----

3   Hebrews 11:4 (*The Message*)

Which is kind of like our middle child, Brittney, who worked for weeks in preschool to give me (Carla) a painted, clay…*thing* for Mother's Day. Was it an ashtray? I doubt it because I don't smoke—I never have. Or was it a paper clip holder? It was tough to tell simply by looking at it sitting there in little Britt's hand. The truth is, it didn't so much matter what *it was*, because it wasn't the object that mattered. When I saw Britt holding the clay "thing," I didn't see an ugly glob of clay painted puke brown.

I saw my daughter's love.

I saw Britt's sweet *heart* that made the *thing* valuable.

Cain went through the motions, but his heart simply wasn't in it. He never got that the *thing* was more about his *heart*. He never got that his relationships with his little brother and with his God were both exposing the condition of his heart. He never got that by keeping his *heart* from God, he was keeping the *thing* God wanted most.

Rather than moving toward God, Cain responded by doing *things* his own way. It was a decision that not only led to his brother lying dead in a field—it was also a decision that led to him stabbing his relationship with God.

The Psycho is at the Door.

//   What can happen when we do the right thing for the wrong reason?   //

We sometimes think of sin as doing the "wrong thing." But even more fundamentally, isn't sin simply closing our hearts to God? Because we can do the right thing for all the wrong reasons. We can "serve" to impress others rather than to genuinely meet needs around us. We can "give" to the poor in order to get something— recognition, admiration, or respect—from the rich.

When our youngest, Casey, turned thirteen, I took her on a rite-of-passage mission trip, as I did with our other kids. While in Kenya, we found ourselves struggling with the tension that we'd taken the trip more for our benefit than for the benefit of the Kenyans. *Were we outwardly doing the "right things,"* we wondered, *for the "wrong reasons" because our hearts were set more on our purposes than God's?*

It was an important question to wrestle with—and one that turns us back toward God—because we often "love" in order to get. We often miss the mark by doing what appears to be the right thing on the outside for all the wrong reasons inside. Not because they're not good things to do, but because we're missing God's original intent for how relationships were created to be.

In one of his letters, as the apostle Paul is writing to a group of people he loves deeply, he gets all soft in the heart and breaks into beautiful, poetic language about what love is and what it isn't. People still gush over it today—"the love chapter,"[4] they call it—and read it at wedding after wedding.

But if you listen carefully, it's also a bit unnerving. In describing the attributes of love, Paul says,

> *If I speak in the tongues of men and of angels, but have not love, I am only a resounding gong or a clanging cymbal. If I have the gift of prophecy and can fathom all mysteries and all knowledge, and if I have a faith that can move mountains, but have not love, I am nothing. If I give all I possess to the poor and surrender my body to the flames, but have not love, I gain nothing.*

It sounds *pretty*, but it's also *pretty harsh*. Because what he's saying is that we can do all those *things*—great things that from the outside look like a Mother Teresa highlight reel—but if we do them our way instead of God's way, Paul says that it amounts to less than some old *thing*. It amounts to *no-thing*.

Nothing.

If I have faith that God can do *anything*, but I don't love—it's *nothing*.

---

4   1 Corinthians 13.

If I give *everything* I own to the poor, it amounts to *nothing* if it isn't done with love.

If I sacrifice my very life by being burned to death, but it's not motivated by love—that's right—it's *nothing*.

Instead it's just a dull, hollow, going-through-the-motions, aimless wandering. And as Cain knows, for those who simply go through the motions, "sin lies at the door... and its desire is for you."

That's a terrifying image. Something straight out of a horror movie. We're just one door away from a rabid beast waiting to rip us limb from limb. Or a deranged killer breathing quietly on the other side. Or, more accurately, Satan in a hockey mask waiting with a spiritual chainsaw behind that door.

It sounds gruesome, but it's true. That reality of sin waiting at the door is *why* God was begging Cain to "do well" and to "rule over" sin. It's the same thing He warns us about—mastering sin.

If we don't, there will be hell to pay.

A Life Lab for Our Spiritual Growth.

//   What is sanctification and how do our relationships nurture it?   //

Relationships are a life lab for our spiritual growth, and this Relationship 101 class reveals how much we miss God's original intent for humanity. The Bible has a word for this transformative work in our lives: *sanctification*. Sanctification is God's process of taking our created and fallen humanity and re-creating it by His Holy Spirit, taking us back to His original intent for us, the image of God. Those tensions of being together with someone you know well and who knows you well are all part of bringing about your sanctification, and no one person on this Earth gets inside that heart that God yearns for as much as your partner.

In his book *Sacred Marriage*,[5] author Gary Thomas asks the question, *what if God designed marriage not to make us happy, but to make us holy?* It's a great question because it challenges our assumptions of what marriage is and what it isn't. He writes, "Everything about your relationship—everything—is filled with prophetic potential, with the capacity for discovering and revealing Christ's character." Deep, meaningful relationships have a way of rubbing the veneer off our imperfections and exposing who we really are. Iron may sharpen iron, as the Proverb says,[6] but it also causes sparks to fly in the process. And in a seriously dating relationship we find that our lives are more and more exposed as we grow in intimacy with our partner. God uses that very pressure from intimate, imperfect relationships to shape us. It's a process that continues into marriage and to the very end of our lives. "One of the best gifts God gave you," Gary and Betsy Ricucci wrote in their book, *Love That Lasts: When Marriage Meets Grace*, "was a full-length mirror called your spouse. Had there been a card attached, it would have said, 'Here's to helping you discover what you're really like!'"[7]

The apostle Paul talks about what that process of sanctification looks like in his letter to the Romans:

> So here's what I want you to do, God helping you: Take your everyday, ordinary life—your sleeping, eating, going-to-work, and walking-around life—and place it before God as an offering. Embracing what God does for you is the best thing you can do for him. Don't become so well-adjusted to your culture that you fit into it without even thinking. Instead, fix your attention on God. You'll be changed from the inside out. Readily recognize what he wants from you, and quickly respond to it. Unlike the culture around you, always dragging you down to its level of immaturity, God brings the best out of you, develops well-formed maturity in you…The only accurate way to understand ourselves is by what God is and by what he does for us, not by what we are and what we do for him.[8]

---

5   Which we highly recommend, by the way. This is the *best* marriage book written to date.
6   Proverbs 27:17
7   Ricucci, Gary and Betsy. *Love That Lasts: When Marriage Meets Grace* Wheaton, IL: Crossway, 2006: 132.
8   Romans 12:1-2, 3b (*The Message*)

Did you catch that last part?

It is not who you are or what you do that catches God's attention. His loving, full attention is already focused on you, so the best offering you can give is, as Abel knew, your life. Your heart—your very self—responding to Him.

You will still feel the inner pull to do things your way instead of God's way, of course, but He doesn't give up on you. God always endeavors to bring us all back on track, working with us where we are, transforming our lives from self*fish*ness to self*less*ness. God even takes our mistakes and, like the endlessly creative artist that he is, incorporates those very mistakes into the masterpiece of our lives to create something fresh and beautiful—with every life, a brilliant new riff on the old theme of redemption.[9]

The Happiest of Endings.

Let's return to what God did with Rowdy and Anna's story, because fortunately for them, questions, time, mistakes, and personal issues forced them to consider their relationship more deeply than they had that night on the beach at Young Life camp and over the months that followed. Here is the beauty that God brought out of the chaos they experienced.

Today, Rowdy survives day to day on the money he makes trading futures. Many days he loses big money—but he has also found that he does not need much to survive. He also works full time for a ministry that mentors inner-city kids after school in a rough, drug-saturated neighborhood. He loves the high risk and rewards that inner-city ministry and the stock market bring, as well as the uncertainty and action that each day drops on him. He is fulfilling his passion to serve Christ in a radical way.

Anna is now married to a wonderful man and teaches in a suburban, Midwestern school near where she grew up. Out of the security that her husband and family bring to Anna, she ministers to high school girls who struggle with self-esteem

9 *Sanctification* is God's process of re-creating us through his Holy Spirit back into his original intent for us, the image of God. Find out more about what it means for the Holy Spirit to sanctify his followers by looking up the following verses: Exodus 31:13, John 17:17-19, 1 John 1:9-10, Galatians 2:20, 1Corinthians 1:2, 30.

issues and eating disorders in a place where appearance is everything, helping them realize that their significance does not come from performance. She is passionate about Midwestern life and her relationship with Christ, and God has brought her a husband who shares similar passions.

You may have expected a "happy ending" for Rowdy and Anna—but indeed it is the happiest of endings (or beginnings), for both of them *have* found God's unique directions for their lives. That "syntax error" that caused them so much grief wasn't merely a bump in the road—it *was* the road they had to travel, twisting and winding though it was. They needed to go through that deep questioning, and any other path could have been a shortcut to potential trouble. As they agonized over the questions, drilling through the layers in search of Truth—an encounter with God Himself—they were able to discern more fully who they really are and where they needed to change individually and in their relationship together.

Like Cain, you can reject what God is communicating to you through your relationships. Or, like Abel, you can respond from the heart to God's work in your life, wrestling to become more as God intended you to be as you seek to know that you know.

Your choice is nothing less that the difference between moving closer to God or wandering from His presence.

//////////////

You don't get wormy apples off a healthy tree, nor good apples off a diseased tree.

The health of the apple tells the health of the tree. You must begin with your own life-giving lives. It's who you are, not what you say and do, that counts. Your true being brims over into true words and deeds.

Why are you so polite with me, always saying "Yes, sir," and "That's right, sir," but never doing a thing I tell you? These words I speak to you are not mere additions to your life, homeowner improvements to your standard of living. They are foundation words, words to build a life on.

If you work the words into your life, you are like a smart carpenter who dug deep and laid the foundation of his house on bedrock. When the river burst its banks and crashed against the house, nothing could shake it; it was built to last. But if you just use my words in Bible studies and don't work them into your life, you are like a dumb carpenter who built a house but skipped the foundation. When the swollen river came crashing in, it collapsed like a house of cards. It was a total loss.

-Luke 6:43-49 (*The Message*)

At the end of each section, we want to slow you down and offer you a way to process your thoughts. Maybe the best thing books do for us is to take us

out of the ordinary routine of life,

and help us to think and reflect.

You have our permission to disagree with us or shake your head at our cheesy lines. We are just being who we are and communicating lessons observed as we have traveled the road with people just like you. We hope, you don't agree with everything we say. Life would be soooo boring if we all approached it the exact same way.

Our intent is that with each question that drives our conversation, you will create another question that will ultimately lead you into deeper understanding, for we want to leave space for these tensions to shape your thinking about marriage.

Now that you are at the end of this section, take time to reflect on how tensions create a beautiful work of harmony. We would suggest identifying an art studio, factory, construction site, or other place of "creative chaos," where something is being constructed. Drop in and observe the various tensions necessary to create the finished product. Look for harmonious elements. Were there more tensions or harmonious elements?

NOTE: In this book we hope to allow the tensions of each question to shape your thinking about marriage.

Should marriage be easy or not? What if, as Gary Thomas suggests, God has an end in mind that goes beyond our happiness and comfort? What if God didn't design marriage to make life "easier"? Do you believe life should be near perfect all of the time, some of the time, or never? What does it mean to be "perfect"?

consider the

///////////////

s_one

section_01
    consider the pressure
///////////////

004 why do I want to be married so badly?

....

The other day our youngest daughter said she has "waited *forever* to get to drive." Fifteen-year-old Casey had watched her older brother and sister drive and felt left out.

Waiting.

Do you remember what it was like to wait before you got your driver's license? Graduate from high school? Turn 21? At the time it probably seemed like forever....

But can you imagine waiting four hundred years, as the Israelites had waited for their release from captivity?

They'd been stuck in Egypt as slaves.

The land promised to them by God seemed like distant history.

And so after over four hundred years, they wondered where God was.

What was He up to?

Then, finally, they got the break they'd been waiting for.

God began applying pressure to Pharaoh by sending Egypt a series of plagues, making it clear that whether or not Pharaoh wanted to let the Israelites go, God had other plans. So *finally* Pharaoh told the Israelites to get out of there. Which is exactly what they'd been waiting for over four hundred years—to get *out* of there and *into* the Promised Land.

And they wanted both *badly*.

To most of us at one time or another, marriage looks like a Promised Land flowing with all kinds of wonderful things: life-long love, the assurance that you'll be there for each other through thick and thin, and a relationship so close that your lives begin to somehow mingle in a wonderful, mysterious oneness.

Who wouldn't want *that*?

Who wouldn't want that *badly*?

When we want something like marriage badly, imagining the "good stuff" in that Promised Land comes is it time to consider moving from commitment to covenant? | p.173 easily. But as the Israelites soon found out—and as you may be finding out as you face tough questions prior to engagement—the difficulties getting from point A to point B can make the journey more than you bargained for.

The truth is that getting there will take some wandering (*How do I know that I know?*). It will probably take some brushes with doubt about whether you're moving forward or backward (*Am I getting any closer to figuring this out?*). It may even take some circling back around, as the Israelites did in the wilderness on their way to the Promised Land (*Didn't I already answer that question?*). Patience with this meandering path can be difficult, and too often we hurry ahead in our minds to that destination we want to reach so badly, forgetting all the ground that lies between here and there.

Like the Israelites in the wilderness, it's easy to grumble.

From God's "big picture" perspective, however, the pressure we experience along the way is part of what makes "the good stuff" of our lives *very good*. For He uses those pressures in our lives to help clarify both where we are and where we're going.

What happens along the journey affects what that destination looks like when we finally get there.

Ring By Spring?

//   What is pushing me to get married?   //

José and Jennifer have been dating for two and a half years.

He's ready to take the next step into marriage.

She's not so sure yet.

But it's not only José's inner desire that is driving him to want to be married so badly—it's the external pressures he's facing as well. It is his mother pushing him toward marriage as if she were a seventh-grade girl pushing a friend onto the floor at a homecoming dance. It's the pressure he feels that if he's not married by his early twenties, everyone in his church will wonder what's wrong with him. It is the pressure he feels from his friends as he approaches his last year of university for Jennifer to have a "ring by spring."

These pressures—both internal and external—all build up, of course.

They push us.

They pull us.

They distract us.

They are like a car riding our rear bumper on the freeway, pushing us to go faster. Sometimes the pressures even drive us to do things we might not otherwise do in our relationship—to slam on the brakes or stomp on the accelerator (in relationship speak, that would be "bail on the relationship in a panic" or "rush to the altar"). Given all these pressures, then, how much of José's "readiness" for marriage is genuine and how much is he being propelled forward by the pressures around him?

More importantly, how much of your wanting to be married so badly is because of those pressures in your life and how are they affecting *you*?

Marriage is No "Get Out of Jail Free" Pass.

//   If it is difficult for you to exercise restraint now, why?   //

Occasionally Carla and I talk with couples convinced they should go ahead and get married so as not to "burn in their lust." What they're usually saying is that sexual pressure is building inside them like a pressure cooker and they don't want to get burned.

Believe me, I understand that inner pressure and think it's great that they want to follow God. I really do. And at first glance, their proposal may seem wise. After all, aren't they following the apostle Paul's admonition that "if they cannot control themselves, they should marry, for it is better to marry than to burn with passion"?[1]

But stop and think about this.

If you find yourself habitually wanting to spend more money than you have, is getting more money going to help your restraint? Or does that sidestep the issue?

----

1   I Corinthians 7:9. In his *New International Commentary on the New Testament, The First Epistle to the Corinthians*, Gordon Fee says, "Paul is not so much offering marriage as the remedy for the sexual desire of 'enflamed youth,' which is the most common way of viewing the text, but as the proper alternative for those who are already consumed by that desire and are sinning." Fee, Gordon *The First Epistle to the Corinthians* (Grand Rapids: William. B. Eerdmans Publishing Co., 1987): 288-89.

In other words, is an inability to control yourself before marriage going to change after you marry?

Well, you may think, *if I have more money (or sex), then my need for either won't be so great.*

Perhaps. But if it is difficult to exercise restraint now, ask yourself, *why*? We're not saying it isn't difficult—it certainly is. But what about all that Scripture says about self-control and love…and how the two are inextricably connected? If you can't control yourself *before* marriage, something will control you *after* marriage. Your passions may control you. Temptation may control you. Someone else may control you. But if you aren't able to control yourself, something else will.

Sex and money are only two things that cause us to want to be married badly, of course. We feel that inner, driving pressure for all kinds of things: security, attention, escape, you name it. And whatever your inner pressure, you may feel that right now you're behind bars, in a kind of jail, with…

nowhere

to

go.

what do I do with this sex-driven life? | p.131

But marriage isn't a "get out of jail free" pass. A ring on your hand won't magically change your discipline and desires. We are not saying that you must have everything together prior to marriage, but in major areas that have a way of controlling us (like sex), it is crucial not to look to marriage as a "cure all." If you're running toward marriage while running away from mastering sin in your life, you'll still eventually end up wandering on the other side.

Pressed from Both Sides You Find the Well-Worn Path.

//   How does the pressure we experience in seeking to "know that we know"
help us find God's path for us?
What does it mean to have peace about the decision?   //

When we feel these pressures, it's easy to believe we missed a turn somewhere. If the relationship is good, why does it sometimes seem so difficult? You might even ask others how you can know that you know whether or not to marry, and some might answer, "Oh, you'll feel a peace about it."

Peace?! you might think. *My pros and cons for getting engaged are fighting in some crazed WWE wrestling match, flipping off the ropes and body slamming each other into the mat! How is that peace?*

Pursuing that peace doesn't mean taking the path of least resistance; peace isn't found by dodging every conflicted, confused emotion. It doesn't come from avoiding those soul-searching questions and trying your best to keep those white-hot, romantic feelings burning, those feelings you felt when you first started dating.

In other words, peace doesn't mean you won't at times feel at war inside.

That's because that deep peace doesn't ultimately come from tying the knot. It doesn't come from having someone to love you more than anyone else in the world or from having someone with you 24/7. That peace isn't found living in the Promised Land of marriage.

In his letter to the Romans, the apostle Paul wrote "since we have been justified through faith, we have peace with God *through our Lord Jesus Christ* [italics mine]."[2] With that foundation of peace with Christ, when we feel those internal and external pressures squeezing us, we can "rejoice in our sufferings, because we know that suffering produces perseverance." And if you're planning on living your

digging your own cisterns? | p.084

2   Romans 5:1

entire lives together through the up's and down's of life, perseverance is a pretty good quality to have.

The apostle Paul goes on, because the benefits go on. When we persevere in our sufferings, our character—who we are—develops. And as we experience God's faithfulness again and again, we understand more and more that He is steering our future in a great direction—even if part of what He must use is the junk we put ourselves through. When we know that God is doing this good work, even though we can't see it, we become people filled with hope because we trust in God's faithfulness.

We suffered while watching our two-year-old son, Bo, go through childhood cancer—but we often say "it was the greatest experience we *never* want to go through again." Why? Well, enduring that ordeal has shaped who we are in ways we could never imagine.

What does this all have to do with the decision to be married? you might ask.

As you pursue that peace rooted in *God*, that faith that He is at work in your struggles and questions, it relieves pressure from seeking that foundational peace through your relationship with your partner—of wanting to be married so badly in unhealthy ways. Your spouse can help meet part of your need—we need others to help us walk through life—but he or she is a poor substitute for God Himself.

As much as we would like him to, Christ doesn't magically replace our hard questions with easy answers. Instead, he patiently tutors us *through* them so that when we finally come up with answers, they too are hard.

Rock hard.

Solid.

Unmovable.

That solid peace withstands the pressures and grows stronger because of them, instead of a hollow peace that exists only because…well, nothing's yet come up against it.

Pay Me Now or Pay Me Later.

//   *If you want to be married so badly, why?*   //

With the cash Carla and I received from our wedding gifts, we had enough money to buy a brand new car. Well…we couldn't exactly "buy it." But we had enough to make a down payment. So we were *buying* it; we just weren't…well, *paying* for all of it.[3] We went down to the dealer and picked the exterior paint, the fabric and interior color, engine size, and the color of the vinyl roof and those "awesome" spoke wheels they had back then.

Hey, it was 1984 after all.

Fast forward several years. We were expecting our first child and money was extremely tight on the *big-time* youth minister's salary we were pulling in each month. (As in, *way* too much month left at the end of the money.) Finances were so tight that during one date we didn't have any money for dinner. Instead we scoured the house for change and even pilfered the car ashtray for enough coins to buy one Dairy Queen Blizzard. (We could actually *buy* that. No installment plan needed.) We *walked* a half mile to DQ, then fought over who got to hold it while we "shared" the Blizzard. You could just feel the love.

Then, with a year and a half left to pay on our car loan, the car's air conditioner went out—and a car without A/C in Central Texas is like a mobile oven. I took the car in for repair and found it was going to take almost eight-hundred dollars to fix. Well, eight hundred dollars in the mid-1980's was as out of reach to us as a million dollars. We didn't have eighty cents, much less eight-hundred dollars.

---

3   Sadly, people today don't seem to have a problem with that distinction, and back then neither did we.

So I had this brilliant idea. Actually a car salesperson had the "brilliant" idea and I bought into it. She showed me how I could trade in my two-year-old vehicle for a brand new Mazda 626 by using the principle we had accrued. Our monthly car payment would even go down. *Unbelievable!* The salesperson was clearly a genius with a brilliant solution and we did not have to pay a dime. (Which was a good thing because we'd already collected all the dimes from under the sofa cushions anyway.)

That was my kind of math.

It sounded brilliant.

It *was* brilliant!

In hindsight, however, it was like having a house with a leaky roof and picking up and moving. Or being too tired to wash your clothes and going out and buying new ones. Now we had a five-year loan instead of paying off our broken-A/C car in only a year and a half. Our quick fix of the A/C problem took us five more years to pay off, and we probably paid ten times more than our original repair estimate.[4]

When you avoid the pressures in front of you, you may enjoy the ease and "benefits" for a time (low monthly car payments), but you only put off a more difficult job for later (many, many more of those monthly payments).

The same is true of the pressures you feel.

If you want to be married *so* badly, stop and ask yourself, *why?*

Why do you feel the things you do?

What are the pressures pushing in on you from the outside?

What are the pressures propelling you from the inside?

---

4   We ended up driving our A/C-solution vehicle, the Mazda, for ten years and almost 300,000 miles—and the A/C went out twice on that one. However, we finally learned our lesson and paid cash for repairs.

Sometimes we feel the drive we do because we're trying to…well, drive away from something else—our own insecurity or lack of affection or feelings of inadequacy. Perhaps we're grasping for something in our partner that's only meant to be found in our relationship with God. Your desire to be married *badly* may be pointing to wounds in your life crying out for attention. You may want desperately to be cherished for who you are, to receive the attention you were denied or the love you needed growing up.

hiding out | p.167

If there is a pressure pointing you toward something in your life that needs looking at, don't look away.

Look it squarely in the eye.

Face it head-on.

What Better Opportunity to Love Greatly?

> //   How does love respond to the pressures that push us toward marriage?   //

Those pressures press us for an answer to the question, *do we really want to be married badly?*

Badly enough to face them head-on and struggle through them to the other side?

Or bad-ly enough that we give in, turn a blind eye to the pressures, and hope that marriage will fix it all?

Which will it be?

Most of us don't know how committed we are—how willing we are to take that step of faith into marriage—until we go through the doubts and questions that press on us from both the inside and outside. Put another way, *as you face those internal and external pressures propelling you to want to be married so badly, you have an opportunity to grow in love.*

And isn't love the very thing you want as you think about marriage?

If love is *patient*, what better opportunity to grow in love than to work patiently through the pressing questions you have, going through the hard work of seeking out wisdom and assessing whether the pressures pushing on you should cause you to slow down?

If love is *self-controlled*, what better opportunity to grow in love than to push through sexual pressure and exercise self control in your physical relationship with your partner?

And if love *seeks the best for others*, what better opportunity to lay down your life for your potential future mate by refusing to let your choice be dictated by the pressures coming at you from friends, family, your church, culture—and from within?

If you do end up marrying, that's the kind of love that will stand up to a lifetime of *up's* and *down's*.

005 why am I so scared to get married?

....

It was a classic case of girl meets boy.

Girl was an independent spirit, a go-getter, the kind of person voted "most likely to succeed" by her high school senior class for her "anything you can do, I can do better" attitude. And she was doing pretty well at succeeding on her do-it-myself course.

Until she met boy.

Now that they're a seriously dating couple and the relationship is working out, he is ready to take the next step into marriage. But she isn't so sure. She's scared of making that kind of a commitment. Afraid, she says, of losing her identity.

Can you relate?

You too may be afraid of losing your identity.

Or you might wonder whether you'll have enough money to survive as a couple.

Or fear making the "wrong decision" regarding the person you choose to marry.

Or of having a relationship like the one your parents had.

Or of simply being miserable.

Fear often keeps us from making bad choices, clueing us in on what we need to avoid and why. But fear sometimes holds us back from making good choices, like when we're in a great relationship, but fear the *what-if*'s.

How then do we begin to distinguish between these two pressures, between the fear that keeps us from making bad decisions and fear that keeps us from making good decisions?

Holy Fear.

//   Could the fear I feel at stepping into marriage be healthy?   //

Once, when I (Byron) was a boy of only six or seven, my dad and I were standing outside in a cotton field. I was on a tractor when suddenly I could see on my dad's face a look of terror. He was trying to get the words out "*stay on the tractor*," but somewhere in that mix he said the word *snake*.

I hate snakes. I always have. And when he said that s-word, I jumped right out of the tractor…which was exactly what he'd told me not to do. It would have been a narrow escape if, as I thought, the snake was in the tractor with me, sitting there curled up on the seat or slithering around my feet down by the pedals.

But it wasn't.

And I landed right next to that big, ole' fat snake curled up on the ground.[1]

It's natural to fear certain things. Poisonous snakes, for example. Being afraid of them is healthy, because bad things can happen when you're around them. Like being bitten. Dying a painful death. Those sorts of things.

---

1   It ended up being a harmless bull snake; a big snake, but a harmless one.

We fear what might hurt us. Scared that if we take another step, the snake will bite. Or that somehow our *partner* will strike. And what hurts more than being rejected by those we love?

Or abandoned.

Laughed at.

Devastated by the very one we love the most.

None of us want that to happen. Taking that step is a bit like big-wave surfing. Sure, it looks fun—and we like imagining ourselves doing it—but people die trying.

That kind of fear isn't pretty.

But it's also natural to feel a kind of fear standing on the edge of marriage, knowing that we are way out of our league. Knowing that we will often fail. There's certainly a positive side to fear, for in Scripture there's something called the "fear of the Lord," which is that awareness that our lives are completely and utterly at the mercy of an all-powerful and Holy God. And as we consider stepping into this thing He's created called marriage, we all at times feel inadequate. That awe, that reverence, that fear is healthy. Frightening, yes, but still very, very good. Because though God is all-powerful, He isn't trying to wipe you out like a wave, or eager to rip you limb from limb like a shark.

It gets even better, because Scripture says that the "fear of the Lord is the beginning of knowledge."[2] If you're trying to know that you know whether or not to get married, *fearing the Lord is the beginning of that knowing.*

Didn't think fear could be so good, did you? But it's true. In the face of that decision of whether or not to step into marriage, holy fear of God and His creation we call marriage is a healthy thing to feel.

---

2   Proverbs 1:7

Into-Me-See.

//   Why is intimacy—being known—so scary?   //

One of the best definitions of intimacy we have heard is…well, just the way it sounds: "into-me-see."[3] When someone sees into who we are, that is intimacy.

If there's any couple who knew about the beauty of intimacy, it was Adam and Eve. The two of them had a great thing going in the Garden of Eden. The Old Testament book of Genesis says that when they got together, they were both "naked and unashamed." In other words, they could be completely open with each other, baring everything—everything they felt, everything they thought, everything they experienced. There was nothing to hide. No feelings of jealousy over who was getting how much of whatever. No wishing they were somewhere else instead of where they were. No playing games. Nothing to hide.

But then a peculiar thing happens. After they do what God told them not to—namely, eating from the Tree of the Knowledge of Good and Evil—Scripture says that their eyes were opened and they saw that they were naked.

Well, duh, you might think. *Didn't they notice that* before?

But think about this for a moment.

It wasn't so much that Adam and Eve suddenly realized that their body parts were hanging out there for all to see.[4] They already knew each others' bodies, after all. Instead, what happened was that they had suddenly become way more concerned with what others might *know.* For the first time in human history, they were aware of all that they didn't want others to know.

The feelings of shame.

Of wanting to withdraw from others' presence.

---

3   We wish we could say we came up with this. But the first time we heard it was during a talk by an amazing youth communicator, Dave Busby, who is now deceased.
4   All two of them plus God.

To hide.

It must have terrified them to experience such feelings for the first time. All they'd ever known in the Garden of Eden was knowing and being known. Then suddenly they didn't want to be fully known—didn't want others to see into them, didn't want "into-me-see."

Since then we've come up with all kinds of things to hide. Jealousy of what others have. Secret addictions. Hatred toward those who have caused us pain. With all that we have to hide, pulling back the curtains and giving someone a clear view inside is scary. It's risky. It's laying your very self on the line—the good, the bad, and the ugly—and waiting to see whether or not you'll be embraced.

how much baggage am I willing to carry? | p.163

And all of us do want to be embraced. We all carry in ourselves that longing to be received just as we are. It's just that after the Fall in the Garden of Eden, "into-me-see" got a whole lot more difficult.

"Perfect Love Casts Out Fear…"

//   How does God's love counteract fear?   //

Most of us don't read the King James Version of the Bible much anymore because the language reads as if Jesus and his disciples are stuck in a Shakespeare play and can't get out. But the translation still occasionally catches a word even in this day and age that makes us sit up and take notice. Here's one from 1 John 4:18: "There is no fear in love; but perfect love casteth out fear; because fear hath torment."

Fear hath *torment*.

That's an interesting way of putting it, but it's true, isn't it? When fear has its way with us, it can torment us, like a sadistic cat batting a crippled mouse back and forth for fun, keeping it alive just long enough to mess with it. When fear torments us, we find ourselves turned inside out by *what-if*'s, by real or imagined pain. We feel as if something's after us, about to do us in.

Tormenting us.

But then there's the other wonderful side to that verse, the *love* part. A great thing happens when we love our partner with a Godly love. That holy love brings the presence of Christ's Spirit into the mix. As we are loved by our partner with the same love that God loves us with, we are helped away from fear.

"Perfect love casteth out fear."

"Perfect" doesn't mean that we should expect ourselves to love flawlessly. We know we can't do that. It's talking about loving with the love of God, who is perfect. And as our egos diminish and Christ's Spirit is allowed to express Himself through us, His perfect love shines through us more and more. As you love your partner and your partner loves you with God's love, fear subsides. Sure, it takes time. And, yeah, we often get in the way. But God still works through us in spite of ourselves.

When you think about it, it's a great reversal of what happened to Adam and Eve. They were cast out of the Garden, but the apostle John says that when the love of God comes back into play, working in us and through us, it is *fear* that is cast out of our lives. And when that happens, it is God's perfect love that "casteth" out fear, woos us from hiding, and back into *"into-me-see."*

Which is just how a good Shakespeare play might end.

006 what do I bring to the table?

....

Carla and I hadn't been dating very long, and I thought I pretty much had her figured out. We were so enamored with our two-dimensional understandings of each other that, like most seriously dating couples early in their relationship, we believed our love was unique in the history of humankind. We would talk for hours during the "mystery dates" I took Carla on (most of them a mystery to me because I was usually making it all up on the fly as we went along), laughing at all the same things, and finishing each others' sentences. It was clear to us that no one since the creation of the world had ever experienced the kind of connection *we* were experiencing.

Amazing chemistry.

Magnetic attraction.

I mean, we were so in synch it was like we were mind-melding.

Fast forward ten years. Carla and I were married and had small children. I planned one of our "mystery dates" with her to remind us of those early days of dating. But while I had my mind set on a weekend of goofing off, I think Carla expected something a little more serious, something a bit closer to fasting and prayer.

The truth is, as much as you may feel in sync with your partner when you're a seriously dating couple, "two becoming one" in marriage doesn't always come easily. You're not going to mysteriously share the same mind. You're certainly not going to always hold the same opinions. At times you may wonder whether you're even sharing the same planet.

But I shouldn't expect to share the same mind as Carla. Because we are so different and because my job as her husband is to love her sacrificially, if there's anyone I need to be sharing minds with, it's Christ. When I come from *that* place of security rather than the "security" of everything needing to click in the relationship, then I have something to bring to the table.

Then I have something to give her.

Others in the Crosshairs.

//   What can we learn from Christ's example about focusing on others?   //

The apostle Paul stressed the importance of having the mind of Christ in his letter to the Philippians when he wrote,

> *If you have any encouragement from being united with Christ, if any comfort from his love, if any fellowship with the Spirit, if any tenderness and compassion, then make my joy complete by being like-minded, having the same love, being one in spirit and purpose.*[1]

This is where a glimpse into other cultures and languages gives us insight into the beauty of what Paul is saying here. When he tells them to be "like-minded" and "one in spirit and purpose," those words in the Greek literally mean "thinking the one thing" and "together-souled."[2]

Thinking the one thing.

Together-souled.

1   Philippians 2:1-2
2   Earle, Ralph. *Word Meanings in the New Testament.* (Grand Rapids: Baker Book House, 1991): 335.

Wouldn't you like that in your relationship? It's a beautiful picture of togetherness… *and Paul's not even talking about marriage.* He's talking about the broader Christian community all relating to one another in the unity of Christ, so living this out in your relationship with your partner is a great place to start.

That doesn't mean you won't have your differences; you're clearly going to have opinions on what lies before you. *But what is your motivation when handling your differences?*

Paul points to the life of Christ.

"Do nothing out of selfish ambition," he says. *"Each of you should look not only to your own interests, but also to the interests of others."*[3] The Greek word in this verse for "look," *skopos,* is where we get our English word *scope,* as in *telescope* or *periscope.* It literally means *to take aim at, to focus in on,* and the picture is of looking at a target from a distance. I've been there, hunkered down behind a hunting scope with the crosshairs on a ten-point buck. And whether you're looking at an animal through a scope or looking through a telescope trying to see another galaxy, that scope brings what is far away into clear focus.

That's important, because others' interests usually do feel far away. Carla's needs often are far from my thoughts. They're not in my scope, you could say. The same is true of my kids' needs or the needs of those mingling around me at my church. They aren't always "in my scope."

To do this, to turn from ourselves, we need the mind of Christ to bring those needs that aren't immediately apparent into our line of sight. Sure, we have to take into consideration our own needs—Scripture says we should consider our own interests—but we are also called to set our minds on the interests of others.

You see, we really don't need training in focusing on ourselves. We've got that down pretty well. All we have to do is whip the gun from its holster and shoot from

---

3   Philippians 2:3-4

the hip to hit our own interests. We're all "trigger happy" when it comes to *that*, and how can we miss? But we do have to take aim at one another's interests.

It's like looking through that scope,

> sighting in,

>> lining up the crosshairs,

>>> setting your gaze beyond yourself,

>>> focusing.

Being Secure in Your Own Skin.

> //   Am I secure in my own skin? Why does that matter?   //

When we focus on those around us, we find that each person brings something to the table of great value.[4] As relationships blend our different strengths, they have a way of helping us better understand the full character of God. For this to happen we must:

- Acknowledge that we have been created with unique gifts and functions
- Appreciate the strengths of the other person and welcome the differences
- Consider conflict and tension as an agent of change

Of course, if you are searching for security and peace in your partner rather than in God, it's difficult to focus the crosshairs on him or her, because you'll find that you're always wanting their crosshairs on you. That's a life-long tension, of course, and sharing the mind of Christ isn't easy. Setting aside our own selfish ambitions

----
4   Genesis 2:18; I Corinthians 12:12-27

and setting our focus on God's interests is one of the most difficult things we'll *ever* humanly do.

How difficult?

In the 1970s, a Harvard professor[5] outlined three levels of moral development, which can be paraphrased as:

Level 1—what is best for me,

Level 2—what is best for my group,

And Level 3—what is best for all of humankind.

He believed that a person cannot skip a developmental stage, but must progress through each one systematically, one at a time. In the first level, *what is best for me*, we respond to authority figures, first under threat of punishment and second by realizing that a certain behavior is in our own best interest. In the second level, *what is best for my group*, we seek to do what will gain the approval of others and follow law and order. These levels demonstrate a progression from concern with self to concern with one's supporting social network. But this professor believed that the majority of adults never reach the third level, a "genuine interest in the welfare of others."

Well, for crying out loud. I may have a PhD in the obvious here, but if there's one thing that's needed for a healthy, mature marital relationship, it's a genuine interest in the welfare of others! If I'm always looking to Carla for security and she's always looking to me, doesn't that create a feedback loop causing the sound system to scream? Instead we have to step off our own stage and put down the mic.

Being secure in your own skin doesn't mean "having it all together." If you think you're even close to having it all together…well, that's proof that you don't.

You will at times waver in your love.

----

5 Lawrence Kohlberg

You will at times grasp for security in your partner.

You will fail.

who am I and why am I in this relationship? | p.083

But for any follower of Christ, looking to God for your security instead of to your partner, having that right foundation is…well, foundational.

There's More to Believing Than Just Seeing.

// What does your belief in God rest on? //

Faced with these pressures, we see where our heart truly lies. *What will we choose? Will we look to God, patiently awaiting His wisdom in response to the pestering questions we have inside, or will we turn down the path of least resistance?*

For the Israelites, their hearts rested on what they could see. As they stood on the shore of the Red Sea watching the Egyptian army bearing down on them, they were terrified. The water was at their backs. The Egyptians were bearing down on them. From all they could see before them, it looked like sure death. They cried out to Moses,

> *"Was it because there were no graves in Egypt that you brought us to the desert to die? What have you done to us by bringing us out of Egypt? Didn't we say to you in Egypt, 'Leave us alone; let us serve the Egyptians'? It would have been better for us to serve the Egyptians than to die in the desert!"*[6]

What they apparently didn't see was their God, still working their salvation. Their leader Moses, however, saw with different eyes, which enabled him to say, "Stand firm and you will see the deliverance the LORD will bring you today."[7] He had faith, the ability to trust—to "see"—God's unseen work before him.

---

6 Exodus 14:11-12
7 Exodus 14:13

Seeing is believing, we sometimes say. But that's not necessarily true. For Moses, *believing was seeing the unseen.* There were things he didn't yet see that he believed, because he knew that God was faithful and working around him. It took this kind of pressure for the Israelites' security to be shown for what it truly was. For them, security lay in their circumstances, what they could touch. For Moses, security lay in God. It's only when we're shaken that we find how strong our foundation truly is. Where it's weak, we'll see the cracks.

What was the difference between Moses and the Israelites?

Both had "done time" in Egypt.

Both wanted badly to get to the Promised Land.

Both of them even "believed" in God.

It wasn't until they saw the waters of the Red Sea parting and passed through that the Israelites saw what Moses had seen through faith—that God was not only *real*, but that He was *really* with them, caring for them, saving them. Pressed on both sides—the Red Sea to one side and the Egyptian army bearing down on them to the other—they found God's path for them.

A path in spite of their doubts.

A path revealing that God had been working.

A path through the pressures.

OH HOLY GOD,

I feel pressure from within and without.
I need hope for the future.
I need confidence in the present.

All of this just seems to bring more questioning.
Why don't you eliminate my questions
by making life easier?

During my probing struggle
help me to be secure in my skin,

and give me enough hope to know
YOU will lead me down a well worn path as
YOU teach me to love.

Keep me alert as to what you are going to do next.

/////////////

Now that you are at the end of this section, take time to reflect on how pressures shape (both good and bad) a couples' outlook on marriage. From time to time, it is just good to enjoy a nice dinner together and watch a movie. Have you seen *My Big Fat Greek Wedding*? It is a movie that has been out for awhile, but we highly recommend watching the movie to see the outside pressures a couple faces in the decision to get married as well as the whole marriage fiasco. Plan a date night but reverse the format…watch the movie, then go eat dinner so you can discuss the pressures.

consider the _pressure

section_02
consider the foundation
////////////////

007 why do I do what I do? why do I want what I want?

....

William Thomas was just an ordinary guy on his way to work early one ordinary November morning when his wife noticed a car sinking in New Jersey's Rahway River.

Which, needless to say, was a bit out of the ordinary.

William rushed to the river's edge and saw a woman stuck inside the vehicle, fighting to keep her head above the water flooding in. And so he plunged into the frigid water.

"I just knew that she needed help," he said after rescuing the woman, "and I just dove in without thinking….And by the grace of God I just made it there and back."[1]

As out of the ordinary as that story may sound at first, we also hear stories like it all the time. It shouldn't surprise us too much, because what we do follows what we believe, whether we're waking for an early morning jog because we believe in our health or whether we're risking our life for the sake of another. You don't willingly put your life on the line unless deep down you sincerely believe in the cause, and you don't willingly embrace the pain of running in circles around the neighborhood unless you truly value the gain that comes from doing so day after day. Nike told us to "*just do it*," but we never really *just* do it. We do what we do because we value it, because we *believe* in it.

Our actions emerge from our values.

1   http://www.lifesaving.com/spotlight/rescues/spotlight111.htm

X Marks the Spot.

// Where do our decisions come from?
What drives us to do what we do? //

But let's be honest. As good as our intentions may be, we don't always act true to our values. We often claim certain values as central to our lives and then turn around and neglect them. I may plan an early morning run with Carla, setting out my running shoes, shorts, and T-shirt the evening before, and yet miss a day or two (but certainly never more than that!). We may even claim to value human life, and then stand by in the crowd—terrified to do anything—while the car sinks into the water with a woman trapped inside because, when it came down to it, we value our life more. And, of course, we can claim to love our partner and then at times act as selfishly as a toddler with a handful of candy.

Which also shouldn't surprise us, for who we *want* to be and who we *are*, are often two completely different things. For example, I (Byron) consider myself an athlete. But in reality, I haven't even competed in beer-league softball in years. As Carla would point out, the older I get the better I was. So although I *want* to still see myself as an athlete…well, the reality is I'm a "has been."

Our value to avoid pain may trump physical gain. Personal preservation may replace self-sacrifice. Our own desires may take precedence over others' needs. When it comes to our actions, our true values will surface and ultimately guide our decisions, especially during times of pressure or conflict. As Scripture puts it, *"Where your treasure is, there your heart will be also."*[2]

But knowing what we truly value is difficult precisely because we may fully believe ourselves to be one thing, when, in fact, we are another. *Do you value your partner because of her warm heart or because of her hot body? Do you value him because he's well respected or because he's making lots of money?*

tear up your list... or at least edit it! | p.103

---

2 Matthew 6:21

Our motives are mixed, of course. We're only human after all. And as confusing as all this may be, and as buried as our mixed motives are, God knows us and keeps digging.

It is in those pressures of life, when the winds begin to blow, that we're better able to see our true foundation.

Pressed to Mean What We Say.

//   How do the pressures we face as we "seek to know that we know" show us where our foundation lies?   //

Perhaps nowhere is this split between our values and our actions more evident than in our intimate relationships, because there our selfishness is uncovered as we grow close. As St. Francis of Assisi once said:

> *A servant of God can never know how much patience and humility is within as long as everything goes well. It is in sudden testings that our "treasure" is revealed. When the time comes that those who should treat you fairly do exactly the opposite—you have only as much patience and humility as you see in yourself in that moment, and no more.*[3]

Seeing our claimed values brought together with our actions in the real world is all part of our life-long process of sanctification, but identifying the split is crucial to making a wise decision of whom to marry. Consequently, you must address the question, *what values do I hold as most central, that serve as my reference point?* Because while you may *say* that your values are one thing, at your *core* your values may come from the world, from friends, or family—even misguided values from within the church—and they will affect how you act and the decisions you make, including the decision of whether or not to be married.

---

3   St. Francis The Admonitions: 15 & 13 quoted in David Hazard's *A Day in Your Presence*. (Minneapolis: Bethany House Publishers, 1992): 57.

Guiding Principles: From the World or from the Word?

//   Are the guiding principles we follow from the
world or from God's word?   //

During our years on staff at various churches, we usually worked with high school and college students. But during one speaking engagement we found ourselves at a marriage retreat where most of the members had been married for much longer than we'd been alive.

As we all shared our stories, we found that many of them had eloped or married at only fifteen or sixteen years old, which—as surprising as it may seem—was much more common half a century ago. One man said that he married when he was seventeen and that his wife was only fifteen. When they went to their county courthouse to get a marriage license, since she was only fifteen they were denied. So they simply went to the next county and told them she was sixteen. "She had a 'birthday party' as we crossed the county line," he told the group.[4]

That's something you won't see much of today, because now the median age for a first marriage is just over 27 years for men and just over 26 years for women.[5] People in *your* home town might value getting married soon after high school; people in another town might value first getting a university education or becoming financially stable before marrying. But like the Pharisees, we often begin adding these values to God's word to create "Biblical" values of our own.

While the winds of culture blow every which way, Biblical principles transcend culture and stand the test of time. We may read the Old Testament warning to keep our bull from goring our neighbor[6] and think, *what on Earth does keeping a bull within its fence have to do with me today?*

---

4   Most of the older people at the retreat shook their heads in agreement like it was no big deal.
5   Popenoe, D. and Whitehead, B.D. *The State of Our Unions* (Piscataway, NJ: National Marriage Project, Rutgers University, 2006).
6   Exodus 21:28-29

I mean, really, what relevance does that have in my life if I don't live among cattle ranchers?

Sure, the specifics change, but if we ignore the central principle of being responsible for our property, we may wind up as guilty as that bull's owner if we don't replace our car's failing brake pads and can't stop at the elementary school crosswalk while the kids are crossing. We may not all have fields in which the poor can gather leftover produce after the harvest, as the New Testament talks about, but that doesn't mean we shouldn't care for the poor today with what we *do* have.

The story *then* reads differently than the story *now*. Specifics change. But the principles remain.

What then are the Biblical principles regarding love and marriage that worked for my great grandfather and that will work for my kids' kids?

Because those are the principles worth basing our values upon.

Give Yourself a Good Brainwashing.

> //   What can help close the gap between our
> claimed values and our actions?   //

We must be honest with ourselves regarding these values we *claim* to hold and the values we *truly* hold at our core, for if we adopt misguided values around us, they can have a profound influence on how we relate to one another and, ultimately, what we decide regarding whom to marry and when. Because our actions emerge from our most deeply held values, it is important that you take time to honestly examine yourself to see where your foundation lies and to embrace Biblical principles, which transcend culture.

We need help to keep us on track. We need something larger than ourselves. Something that can steer us back when we inevitably stray from God's intention for our relationships. And if you've been in a church for any length of time, you've probably heard people say that it's important to "spend time in the word." Which, translated from the Christian-ese, simply means, *read the Bible regularly.*

To some, this might sound a bit like brainwashing. Which, in a way, is exactly what it is. *Not mindless-repetition-until-I-can't-think-of-anything-else* brainwashing. Not *read-the-Bible-because-someone-told-me-to-so-I'm-gritting-my-teeth-and-doing-it.* But rather brainwashing as washing what has truly become dirtied. Brainwashing because our minds are covered by the grime of those misguided values we hold deep inside.

Those values need cleansing.

They need to be reworked from our botched attempts at defining them.

They need to be redefined through God's perspective.

As I daily submit my life to Christ, my mind becomes more like His mind. I'm going where he wants me to go; I'm meeting whom he wants me to meet; I'm responding in healthy ways in my relationships. How do we begin to wrap our minds around this? Ask yourself these questions:

- Who is an authority in my life?
- Am I depending on what other people are saying about me for my sense of worth?
- Where do I get my value system from?
- Is God in control of my life? Every area?

And if God's word has authority over our lives, that equips us, enables us, empowers us, and fuels us with the tools we need to see rightly and relate to one another in the way He originally intended us to.

Values Reformation: From Depravity of Self to Faith in God.

He came from the lineage of one of the world's most infamous murderers.

Before he was born, one of his descendants butchered a brother and, as a result, was ostracized from the rest of the family. You don't need a PhD in psychology to see what's coming down the line for this family. Like most stories about someone who grows up in a rough neighborhood as an outsider, our man turned bad himself, following the values of his day...which, needless to say, weren't all that great. Scripture says of that time and place that "the LORD saw how great man's wickedness on the earth had become, and that every inclination of the thoughts of his heart was only evil all the time."[7]

Which doesn't leave a lot to cheer about.

But then something wonderful happened.

Enoch had a radical shift in his foundation. A *conversion*, you could call it. *Repentance*. When we think of repentance, we may think of sweaty, badly-dressed TV evangelists jabbing their fingers in the air and telling us all to "*R-E-P-E-N-T!*" But to repent simply means having a change in orientation back to God, to say *yes* to God when before we had been saying *no*. And so Enoch repented, turning 180 degrees to meet God, who was there waiting to change his life. As a result, Enoch walked closely with God for the remaining 300 years of his life. He walked so closely with God, Scripture tells us, that He whisked him from this life, bypassing death altogether.

Enoch's heart was transformed.

His life from then on was changed.

And his values were never the same.

7   Genesis 6:5

008 who am I and why am I in this relationship?

....

There's a magazine ad that shows a young guy standing in a field on his family's Midwest farm, and he's holding a company's software package to learn to speak Italian.

"He was a hardworking farm boy," the ad copy reads.

"She was an Italian supermodel."

"He knew he would have just one chance to impress her."

We knew a guy like that. Out of his league with the woman he was with. Mismatched. Speaking a different language, you could say. He'd met the gal of his dreams…and that was precisely his problem.

It's a problem a lot of guys I know would love to have, but it was a problem nevertheless because she really was the gal of his *dreams*, not his *reality*—and who we dream we are and who we actually are, are often completely different things. He saw her as someone he probably never had a chance with, and he was probably right. But she expressed an interest in him *(What…you're saying I have a chance?)* and that fueled his fantasies. Sometimes, to realize those fantasies of ours, we become someone we're not. Which is precisely what he did. He wore a mask to win her over.

He didn't set out to deceive her, of course. He simply began trying to live a life that wasn't really his, telling her that he had one more year of college before entering law school. Which sounded great to her. And sounded even better to him.

But it simply wasn't true.

He wanted to believe he was on his way to becoming a powerful lawyer because… well, he also wanted to believe he had a future with this woman. In his mind, the only way to win her over was to jump into a phone booth and become a Superman for the supermodel. In time, he began to believe his stories himself. Who he really was on the inside and who he tried to appear to be on the outside were moving further and further apart. Which would have made for a great screenplay…but it just didn't play out well in real life.

The whole drama raised the question, *who was he really, and why was he in the relationship?*

Are You Digging Your Own Cisterns?

//   How do we go about fulfilling our desire to be significant?   //

We all wear masks at times, trying to come across as someone that we're not. Someone more intelligent. Someone more spiritual. Someone heading down a more exciting path than the one we're on. And because we want people to see "the best we have to offer," sometimes we try to appear that we're a person we aren't in order to gain others' approval. Which is natural, of course. But we flirt with danger when we begin building our identity on something false, when we begin to believe these masks of ours are, in fact, who we really are.

Halfway through college, I (Carla) was pretty sure I had my life together. I was getting good grades. I was investing in good, healthy relationships. I felt successful in so many ways, but largely because my identity was wrapped up in the things I was doing.

The equation went something like this:

$$\frac{Hours\ I\ read\ my\ Bible}{the\ number\ of\ mornings\ I\ woke\ early\ to\ spend\ time\ alone\ with\ God} = measure\ of\ my\ spirituality$$

Essentially, the question that drove me was, *how spiritual was I being through the things I thought I ought to be doing?* It's a question that drives many of us, and for a while I felt I was doing pretty well at measuring up to my own criteria.

But then I went to work at camp the summer between my sophomore and junior years of university. Arriving there was like stepping into a room for an audition and seeing hundreds of people more suited to the part than I was. When I stood there face to face with those who met my criteria better than I did, I plummeted on my self-made bell curve of worth. Everybody there seemed smarter and more spiritual. If they were surpassing me at my own standard, what did that mean about who I was?

The simple answer began to look increasingly like this:

Others > Me

In his book, *Search for Significance*, Robert McGee points out some of the false beliefs in which we put our identity:[1]

- the performance trap (my identity lies in what I do or do not do in meeting certain standards)
- the approval addiction (my identity lies in whether or not others value me)
- the blame game (my identity lies in my belief that those who fail are unworthy; I must attempt to be above failure at all costs)

---
1   McGee, Robert S., *The Search for Significance: Seeing Your True Worth Through God's Eyes.* (Nashville: Thomas Nelson Publishing, 2003).

- the shame game (my identity lies in my remorse over how I've failed—I am what I am; I cannot change; I am hopeless)

All four are ways we grasp for our identity and worth instead of holding onto God's definition of where our worth lies.

Which is exactly what the nation of Israel did. They had turned from God. Surrounding countries were gaining in power—Babylon to one side, Egypt to the other. Things didn't look good. And so the prophet Jeremiah wrote these words, pouring out the heart of God toward His people:

> My people have committed two sins: They have forsaken me, the spring of living water, and have dug their own cisterns, broken cisterns that cannot hold water.[2]

In the desert, where water is extremely precious, by looking for their identity outside of their relationship with God, the people of Israel had metaphorically given up a bubbling spring of water for hollowed-out rocks to hold their own collected water. They were holding onto stale, muddy water when they could have had fresh, crystal-clear water running 24/7.

Not the best trade.

But it's one we all make from time to time. Rather than taking our cues on who we are from God, our "spring of living water," we often create lifeless, stagnant, external criteria based on what we do, how we look, how we talk, and who values us.

The shallow stuff.

The superficial stuff.

All that mask and make-up stuff.

2   Jeremiah 2:13

To understand yourself, then, you have to peel off your mask and honestly scrutinize your habits, your ideals, and your beliefs. If you're aware that you grasp for security in your relationships, you might need to take measures to avoid seeking it from the guy you're with. If you measure yourself by how good-looking the woman is with you, what does that say about where your identity lies?

You see, there's a deeper, more foundational question to ask yourself than, *should we get married?* As author and educator Parker Palmer put it, "the deepest vocational question is not 'what ought I do with my life?' It is the more elemental and demanding 'Who am I?'"[3]

Because how can someone get to know who you are if, with all the masks you're wearing, you don't even know who you are yourself?

You Complete Me—What Does?

//   Does my future mate somehow complete me?   //

Songs proclaim it.

People love it.

It makes for dramatic dialogue in movies.

It's that stupid line *"you complete me."* It sounds so romantic, doesn't it? *You complete me.* It's that mistaken idea that a part of us is missing until we find our spouse.

All of us are indeed searching for completion, for what was lost in the Fall. We are looking desperately for what Adam and Eve once had in the presence of God: significance, a meaningful place in life; security, a safe place; and belonging, a satisfied place.

You're not alone in *that* search.

----

3   Palmer, Parker J. *Let Your Life Speak: Listening for the Voice of Vocation*. (San Francisco: Jossey-Bass, 2000): 15.

But completion simply can't be found in your partner. You can't know *who* you are until you know *whose* you are—until you know your God and what He has done for you. That is where your significance, security, and belonging lie. They're not found in what you do or what you have or who you're in relationship with. Instead, they're found in who you are according to what God has done for all of us.

That love—*God's* love—is the love that brings us completion. You must grasp this, but unfortunately many don't. The author Henri Nouwen wrote,

> This sounds very simple and maybe even trite, but very few people know that they are loved without any conditions or limits. This unconditional and unlimited love is what the evangelist John calls God's first love. "Let us love," he says, "because God loved us first" (1 John 4:19). The love that often leaves us doubtful, frustrated, angry, and resentful is the second love, that is to say, the affirmation, affection, sympathy, encouragement, and support that we receive from our parents, teachers, spouses, and friends. We all know how limited, broken, and very fragile that love is.[4]

So is your identity grounded in your partner? Or in your God? Those are important questions to wrestle with because where your identity is grounded will dramatically impact your ability to achieve healthy intimacy with other people. When teaching on the basics of relationships, Drs. Les and Leslie Parrott begin each session by saying, if you try to find intimacy with another person before achieving a sense of identity on your own, all of your relationships become an attempt to complete yourself.[5]

Which puts an awful lot of pressure on your future mate.

Which creates an awful lot of stress between the two of you.

Which can create an awful lot of problems in your relationship.

---

4   Nouwen, Henri. *In the Name of Jesus* (New York: Crossroad Publishing Company, 1989): 25-26.
5   Parrott, Les and Leslie. *Relationships: An Open and Honest Guide to Making Bad Relationships Better and Good Relationships Great.* (Grand Rapids: Zondervan Publishing House, 1998): 20.

Until you take a good, honest look at who you are, and are okay with what you see, it is very difficult to let others into your life. When you don't want to look into yourself because you don't like what you see, allowing others to see into you *("into-me-see")* becomes extremely difficult.

Moral Maturity.

//   How much does my age matter in taking the step into marriage?   //

It takes time to know who you are, and most people in our culture are still figuring out who they are at least into their early twenties. Unfortunately our culture extends this process into our late twenties or early thirties.

Judging by the way people drive on the freeway, some never figure it out.

Throughout history, people have typically moved from childhood to adulthood through some type of "rite of passage." But we got cheated. Our Western culture has replaced any rite of passage with what we call "going through adolescence." Children are forced to grow up more quickly, yet many of us refuse to *ever* grow up and are instead left with this strung-out stage of wandering and wondering,

of trying to figure out just who we are,

while we're captured and held captive,

for years, if not decades.

The ancients and most people groups today around the world who practice rites of passage into adulthood might laugh as they look at us. *How ludicrous to waste such a life*, they might think. No wonder so many of us find ourselves relying and returning to others—usually parents or grandparents—for the basics of life. Parents like it this way, because they can control you. (We don't consciously say that, but in reality that is what is happening.) You hate the control, but really find yourself with no options.

Let us offer a suggestion that might be freeing.

Our long-time buddy Walker Moore is a youth culture expert with thirty years of experience and way too many pizza-fueled "lock-ins." Somewhere among the teenage madness, Walker latched onto something by studying the "ancient paths" (Jeremiah 6:16) instilled deep within us by our Creator. As he researched and observed our culture, he discovered that we've lost the tools to help individuals move from childhood to adulthood by becoming capable, responsible, and self-reliant.[6] So be on guard for childish incompetence, irresponsibility, and dependent behavior in your partner, because who wants to marry that? We would hate to see any of you holding the leash (you know those awful child leashes you see in the mall) of your dependent partner.

Although experts in the 1980's suggested (heavily suggested) compensating for this trend by marrying later in life, the reality is that age really doesn't matter—it's maturity that counts. And maturity doesn't always come naturally with age. I (Byron) would tend to argue that once a person is capable of biological reproduction, their inner moral core *should* be just as developed. In theory, that is. But our Western culture simply does not facilitate that kind of development. Instead it holds us captive, controlling us to act and think as children—just the way our system wants us to act and think. (Which sounds a bit like being stuck in a low-budget sci-fi movie, doesn't it?) But Walker reminds us that finding our "true identity in Christ, and becoming the capable, responsible, self-reliant adults God designed us to become"

...empowers us to be who we are

and to be free.[7]

6   Moore, Walker. *Rite of Passage Parenting: Four Essential Experiences to Equip Your Kids for Life.* (Nashville: Thomas Nelson, Inc., 2007).
7   Moore, Walker. *Rite of Passage Parenting: Four Essential Experiences to Equip Your Kids for Life.* (Nashville: Thomas Nelson, Inc., 2007):

Are You Man or Woman Enough to Handle It?

//   How do you know when you're an adult?   //

You know you're becoming an adult when you question for the first time whether 99¢ burgers are really something to get excited about. Your favorite band puts out a "greatest hits" compilation. And you no longer say to your friends at 11p.m., "So what do you guys want to do tonight?"

Seriously, *how do you really know when you're an adult?*

When Carla and I are searching for answers to life's questions we often look to the model of humanity, Jesus. Reading about his life, we find several "marks of adulthood" that did not exist during his childhood. His conduct in the book of Luke[8] help us see that in response to hard questions he is able to think and communicate about important life issues, without getting caught up in childish games.

Later in his life, we see several other marks that identified Jesus' maturity:[9]

His conduct was acceptable and appropriate;

he considered others as more important than himself as he made decisions;

and he was trusted to fulfill what he said he was going to do.

Jesus' entire life was to give a correct opinion of who God is. And as *we* mature, that same integrity should increasingly mark our character as well. For if you're going to love someone for the rest of your life, doesn't it make sense to be able to be mature and to take responsibility not only for your own life, but to look out for others as well?

---

8   Luke 2:41-52
9   Philippians 2

In other words, to *grow up.*[10]

But I am not sure the world around us really wants that maturity, that independence. Because who knows? If we are mature, we might change the world.

When you know yourself—when you know who you are and whose you are—it makes an enormous difference in "knowing that you know." Because then…

…you

know

you.

---

connect with **God**

/////////////

> You're blessed when you're content with just who you are—no more, no less. That's the moment you find yourselves proud owners of everything that can't be bought....You're blessed when you get your inside world—your mind and heart—put right. Then you can see God in the outside world.

> -Matthew 5:5 & 8 (*The Message*)

Now that you are at the end of this section, take time to reflect on your core values and how those shape your foundational assumptions of a healthy relationship. As we have discussed up to this point, it is vital to "know thyself" and be secure with who you are before you enter into a serious committed relationship. We encourage you to pull away, go to *that* place of retreat where you do your best thinking, and journal about your essential life values. What is it you believe to be true about life? What drives you? Motivates you? Helps you determine right or wrong? How do these influence your current relationship? Do your actions match your beliefs? Over the next couple of weeks watch to see if your actions match these beliefs.

consider the_foundation

section_03
consider the expectations
//////////////

....

Expectations.

Can't live with them.

Can't live without them.

We all have them, whether they're written down or floating around in our head.

Expectations in the form of a *"things I am looking for in a mate"* list.

You know, those lists that leaders have their high school kids compose at summer camp during "the relationship talk." We're supposed to review that list from time to time and remind ourselves, *if I want to marry a queen, then I have to become a king.* Or something like that.

But let's face it. If we're honest with ourselves, no one ever makes the grade. Not even Jesus would make the cut on many of our lists:

- smokin' hot body (and we know for a fact that Jesus didn't have a hot body)[1]
- rich, but down to earth (by humbling Himself to come in the form of a man Jesus was certainly "down to earth," but he wasn't exactly materially rich)

....
1   Isaiah 53:2

- smart, but not smarter than me (and, well, having created the universe, Jesus probably *is* smarter than you)

In some way, we all create these mental lists. But often our expectations have little to do with reality and much to do with our fantasies. Consequently, an awful lot of bogus criteria often end up on those mental lists of ours.

On the university campus, for example, certain frat guys can only go out with girls from certain sororities. Crazy, I know, but those social rules can feel very *real* at the time. Unfortunately, our list often drives our motives and behavior. *Why?* How important is it that he is part of that fraternity? How important is it that her proportions come as close to Barbie's as possible?[2]

On one hand, having a mental list is not such a bad thing. If you're wondering about whether the person you marry should be a Christian or not and you are a Christian…well, marrying a Christian is a good criteria to have on your list. Scripture supports that thinking.[3] The more differences you have, the more you will have to negotiate and compromise. But taken as the primary gauge for figuring out whether or not you and your partner should be together for life, mental lists aren't enough.

Take, for example, the list from a friend of ours which she made at a 9th grade youth retreat on relationships regarding what she wanted her husband to be.

- 6'2"
- Wavy, dark brown hair…not too short, but not too long either
- Has at least 3 items from Urban Outfitters and 2 from Banana Republic (for dressy occasions) in his closet
- Grew up in Texas
- Has more than one sibling
- Close to his parents, but not too close.

---

2   If Barbie were a real person, her proportions would make her measurements an impossible 36-18-38.
3   For example, Paul's advice in 1 Corinthians 7:39, 2 Corinthians 6:14-16.

Comparing petty similarities and differences, like the kind of music or movies we enjoy, whether to relax or stay busy, or the friends we hang out with, are much less important than the stuff that will get you through your differences going into marriage and those you'll face throughout your years together: Godly character, authentic relationships, the ability to communicate and resolve conflict, and the humility to lay down your life for the other person when those differences present themselves. When those kinds of qualities are part of who you are, you will naturally be attracted to and attract people with similar character attributes. You can't avoid differences altogether by perfecting your compatibility lists, but you must face how you're able to handle your inevitable differences in a respectful manner.

If you don't, the expectation that you match each others' lists becomes absurd when you pursue the wrong-minded notion of searching for Mr. Right.

Looking for Mr. or Mrs. Right?

// Are we right to look for Mr. or Mrs. Right? //

As a committed follower of Christ, my friend Kyle had his own ideas of what he was looking for in a mate.

Enter Jen stage right.

They were the perfect couple, or what we call at our university "Bobby and Betty Baylor." Kyle had movie star good looks and Jen was a "Baylor Beauty." I am serious. At Baylor they actually have such a thing—you make the yearbook and everything. They belonged to the "right" fraternity and sorority. If there had been paparazzi on Baylor's campus, Kyle and Jen would have been at the center of the media attention. Jen is a Godly young woman and as near perfect as a man could ever hope for. Loves people. Loves God. She exceeded Kyle's list.

You get the idea.

But as their relationship began to deepen and move into that lifelong forever phase, Kyle began rethinking a lot of stuff in his personal and spiritual life.[4] The mental list that had brought him so much comfort before in thinking about his dating relationships no longer seemed helpful. After all, Jen not only met his list, but added to it. So he began asking God what *His* perspective was. As he started asking these hard questions—whether his ideas were truly the heart of God or self-made—it started becoming clear that he and Jen were on slightly different pages about their future direction. Small but significant philosophical and theological differences began to emerge. Plus, Kyle was at an unusual place in his life as he discovered new insights about how he related to God.

He sat on our back porch for hours chatting with us about his quandary with Jen, his list, and his relationship with God. He cared deeply about Jen and could not figure out exactly what was going on inside him. She was perfect, his list seemed perfect, but….

For Kyle, the deconstruction and reconstruction of his relationship with God was the easy part. Sure, it took time for him to come to grips with how to "do church" and live in community. But I am convinced that one of the first steps was for Kyle to relinquish control and allow God to show His sovereign power in the complexity of an intimate personal relationship. To see things as God sees them—not in the boxes Kyle wanted to keep things in.

To add drama, Kyle developed a crush on one of Jen's good friends.

To add a plot twist her name was also Jen.

Go figure.

The new Jen (actually "Old Jen" because she was Kyle's best friend's little sister—thus he really knew her longer) was an adventuresome go-getter. Ironically, she had been wrestling with many of the same theological issues as Kyle. The more conversations they had, the more Jen captured Kyle's heart. The two of them took

---

4   You can read about Kyle Lake's process in his book *Understanding God's Will: How to Hack the Equation Without Formulas.*

a leap of faith, started hanging out, and the rest, as they say, is history, for on May 30, 1998, Kyle Lake married Jennifer Gornto.

When we hold onto our "perfect" lists, we not only limit our partner to our narrow, often self-centered criteria; we set an impossibly high standard for him or her to attain. Neither one is helpful. Not to mention we limit the powerful work of God in teaching us valuable lessons from previous relationships.

The things Kyle learned changed him from the inside out.

Both Jens learned valuable things about themselves and God.

And all of them grew.

Tear Up Your List…Or At Least Edit It!

//   If I do have a mental list, what should I do with it?   //

Let's leave Kyle's story and go back to our lists of expectations. We too often focus on each other's "veneer"—that thin, polished, surface layer—thinking it will provide us with all we need to make our decision a life lab for our spiritual growth | p.036 about marriage. But instead of asking, *does he make my list*?, or *how does she score*?, tear up your mental lists. If we expect our partner to meet 100% of our needs, we'll be disappointed 100% of the time.

Instead of focusing on the veneer—the external appearances, earning potential, style—focus on criteria closer to the heart:

Character.

Values.

Similar calling and direction.

Personal beliefs about God and life.

If you must have your list, don't hold it as sacred writing. As inspired as parts of it may feel, it probably isn't the *Bible on What You Need in a Spouse*. What you thought you just *had* to have might need to be replaced. We're not saying that shared interests aren't important; they certainly are. But, unfortunately, so many people today base their decision to marry on such criteria as whether or not they enjoy the same kinds of movies or sports or, yes, belong to the *right* fraternity or sorority.

You see, it's natural to want someone who will fill our longings, yet many of those longings lead us to who we *think* we need, not who we *really* need. At some point, most of us want to marry someone with—let's be honest—superhuman traits. Men would love their woman to have the body of a supermodel, the culinary skills of a top chef, and the spirituality of Mother Teresa. Many women look for a "spiritual leader," a priest of sorts to mediate their spiritual life, a rugged yet emotionally sensitive risk taker, and a six-figure-income CEO. But these idealistic expectations are usually rooted more in the desire for a kind of savior than a kind friend to help encourage us toward our Savior.

As you can see from Kyle's story, even when both people are pursuing authentic character over veneer, minor issues can "red flag" a relationship. God has a way of rewriting even our best scripts, for even minor issues during dating sometimes become major in marriage.

It's crazy, of course, to think that we'll have everything together before we get married. do you have your stuff together? | p.200

If we waited until we were perfectly healthy, we'd never marry. We may be attracted to someone's godliness as well as their goods. We may have one foot on security in Christ and one foot in the financial or emotional security that our relationship brings us. It's natural for us to be attracted to someone for what they bring to our lives—what "tool" they can be for us. You know, a really handy man like the dude on *Extreme Makeover* or a gal who can cook like Giada De Laurentiis. But loving someone for their form and function in your life isn't the same as loving them for their core.

That's why it's important to ask the right questions.

Clarifying Expectations—Asking the Right Questions.

> //   What are the questions I'm asking of my relationship?
> Are they the right ones?   //

There's no such thing as a bad question, teachers often say to their students, which may be true when it comes to our education. But when it comes to making major life decisions, if the questions we're asking take us in a direction we shouldn't be heading, we may find ourselves far down the road, somewhere we never intended. If we're not asking the right questions of our serious dating relationship, we can continue to perpetuate our idealistic expectations, leading us astray.

What are the questions you're asking of your relationship? Are they questions about your partner's veneer? Or are they questions about what lies deep beneath the surface? Your answers are important, because when you are making decisions that will affect the rest of your life, there *are* such things as bad questions.

We wish we could make a list for you list-makers of just-the-right questions to ask God, yourself, your close friends, and family. But because everyone is different, each person's questions will be unique. Thankfully, like a teacher encouraging students to ask questions, God helps us ask *good* questions when He says in the New Testament book of James, "If any of you lacks wisdom, he should ask God, who gives generously to all without finding fault, and it will be given to him."[5]

Wisdom.

True insight into life.

----

5   James 1:5

So while we'd like to give you a list of ten great questions to ask God, we bet that God knows better than we do the questions to ask *you* when you begin asking *Him* what you need.

Expect the Unexpected.

//   Am I willing to set aside my expectations for God's unexpected work?   //

"Expect the unexpected," I (Byron) sometimes tell students, because God is in the business of doing the unexpected. When we lay aside our preconceived expectations and yield to what God is up to, He has a way of showing up and working His sanctification in our lives.

That is exactly what Kyle did when he met and married the new Jen. Kyle and Jen Lake were the perfect couple to pastor UBC,[6] a church that does an excellent job of helping disillusioned college students embrace the Christian faith instead of walking away from it. If ever I have seen a man "called" to a church, it was Kyle's call to UBC, for he provided a safe place for people to deconstruct their faith.

As Kyle changed his focus from his mental list and culturally created expectations to asking God the hard questions, God did an amazing work in his life, in Jen's life (actually, in the lives of both Jens), and in the life of their church community. As a result, faith, hope, and love grew all over the place. That faith step of his was the kind that "makes life worth living," as the New Testament book of Hebrews says. "It's our handle on what we can't see."[7] And it certainly provided Kyle a handle on what he couldn't yet see.

It is precisely that kind of step that Abraham took when he left Ur for the Promised Land.

> The kind of step he took believing God's call to become the father of many nations.

----

6   www.ubcwaco.org
7   Hebrews 11:1 (*The Message*)

The kind of step he ultimately took when he placed his son on the altar before God.

Having the luxury of looking back sure gives us the confidence to trust God with decisions that sometime don't make any sense. It is amazing to see how God used a painful process to do an amazing work in Kyle, Jen, and Jen's life. The other Jen married a dynamic young man and they now have two beautiful children. She cannot imagine being married to anyone other than her husband and is so grateful that a sovereign God walked with her every step of the way.

God's "best" for our lives may not be what we initially perceive it to be. But when we are willing to allow Him to work through us—when our eyes are focused on our Creator and not our created list—we will see His faithfulness. Byron and I know how painful shattered dreams and expectations can be, but even through the hurt God teaches us about Himself. All the stories we have heard over the years have taught us to trust God even more.

Like Abraham and Kyle, we can't see the future. We don't know what it will bring.[8] Be careful, then, that you're not clinging to your list when God shows up to do the unexpected. As Abraham experienced, the path God leads you on just might impact generations and generations to come. I fully expect Kyle's influence will do the same.

You never know.

---

8   Kyle and Jen Lake never dreamt that on October 30, 2005, Kyle would be electrocuted as he stepped into the baptismal waters at his church. Jen's widowed life will never be the same...but then again after Kyle came along, Jen has never been the same.

010 how do I move beyond cultural superficiality?

....

Several years ago, while taking our son on his rite-of-passage mission trip, we had a day off in Spain. As we walked around the port city of Malaga, taking in the local culture, we saw what looked like a stadium. Since Bo was really into soccer at the time, it made sense to go catch a game of real European *futbol*. But as we got closer, I realized it was a historical bullring.

Since bullfighting is a symbol of Spanish culture, I thought it would be a great experience for us to grab tickets. We found an open gate, but as we walked in a man began speaking Spanish to us.

Bo and I were both clueless as to what he was saying.

The situation was classic as the man and I began to speak more slowly and loudly with each sentence. When I realized we were not getting anywhere, I spotted a poster advertising the bull fight, walked him over to it, and pointed. He launched into a rapid explanation that I did not understand a word of. But then I remembered my high school Spanish 1 class. (Or at least one vocab word of it.)

"*¿Dónde?*" I asked.

And the Spaniard must have thought way back to his English I class, because he smiled and said with confidence, as if we had been communicating fluently the entire conversation, "The bull es broke."

I looked at him, then turned to Bo, puzzled.

"The bull is broken?" I said to the Spaniard.

He nodded his head and smiled. *Si*. Bo and I were more confused than ever. Well, since "the bull was broke," we left thinking that the one bull they used must have been injured. But as we walked away and saw the state of the arena, we finally realized with a laugh that it was under construction and that our friend was trying to tell us that the bullring needed repair.

Culture.

It is all around us. Its pull is almost irresistible. And escaping culture's influence can be as difficult as escaping the air we breathe. There are many wonderful aspects to culture: beautiful, moving art and ideas that make the world a better place. But culture can also provide background noise to distract you as you journey to "know that you know," voices around you such as those from the church: *How could I ever marry someone with a sexual past?* Or those from the world: *Why not move in together before we marry to try things out?*

These clamoring messages can drown out God's steady, gentle whisper. And sometimes culture influences us to make decisions we wouldn't normally make otherwise. Cultural values swirling around us can have a profound influence on our relationships, including whom we decide to marry and our expectations within that relationship. And many of those cultural values we base our decisions on—including those values within the church—have little or nothing to do with Scripture.

Which isn't anything you don't already know…but that doesn't necessarily make those values around us any easier to resist.

> *Cultural expectations are difficult to identify and even harder to break.*

Even the Best of Us Struggle With Cultural Expectations.

//   How does our culture get in the way of "knowing that we know"?   /

In the New Testament book of Hebrews,[1] where those who have demonstrated faithfulness are honored, Abraham is given more press than any other character in the entire Bible. Many scholars even refer to him as the Biblical "hero of faith."

Yeah, he's that good.

But maybe not for the reasons you think.

Abraham, formerly known as Abram, didn't start out as the poster child for faith. Like all of us, his trust in God had to grow. And when Abram's faith in God, his "assurance of things unseen," became *un*-sure, his personal and cultural expectations sometimes got the better of him and he began doing things his own way.

Case in point. After Abram and his wife, Sarai, arrived in the Promised Land, God told him that he was going to have descendants as numerous as the stars. God even revealed how it would happen—that Abram would have, as God put it, "a son coming from your own body." But there seemed to be a catch. His wife, Sarai, couldn't get pregnant. It wasn't because of lack of effort—they must have tried and tried. Months slipped by into years, and they surely began to wonder:

Again that question, *what in the world is God up to?!*

Whatever else He was up to, God was refining Abram's and Sarai's faith. You see, like all of us, when he began to doubt God, Abram began to revert to his cultural expectations. And so, when it seemed that it was impossible for Abram and his wife, Sarai, to produce a son, she gave him her maidservant to marry, and Abram had a child through her.[2]

---

1   Hebrews 11
2   As one commentary put it, "It was understood that in this case the wife, and not the mother, had jurisdiction over the child, whose right of inheritance was uncertain until he was legally adopted. When Sarai suggested that Hagar might become the substitute mother of her child she was, therefore, following a socially acceptable precedent…." Baldwin, Joyce G. *The Message of Genesis 12-50*. (Downers Grove: Inter-Varsity Press, 1986): 58.

Abram and Sarai were products of their culture.

Saying *yes* to those around them.

Rather than seeking what God was asking them to say *yes* to.

Going With Culture?

//   Am I going with the cultural flow as I make decisions?   //

Just as Abram turned to his culture for a way to "make things happen" the easy way, in today's consumer society, where online dating can make mate selection seem like point-and-click shopping, we can too easily sidestep the good, hard work of growing in intimacy when the going gets tough in a relationship to instead browse someone else's online profile and rekindle our illusions of "the perfect mate."

But mate selection isn't the iTunes Store.

As Abram experienced, it's often easier to look for cultural "solutions" than push through the difficult work of trusting God and His ways. So how can you know whether you or your partner are caught up in culture? Ask yourself, *are we looking first to God and His principles as revealed in Scripture?*

Or are we taking our cues from the world around us?

I (Byron) was relaxing in front of the T.V. at our house one evening, watching a documentary featuring a group of tribal elders who were sitting in a circle on stumps and old lawn chairs, discussing what the "bride price" should be for a particular young woman.

Talk about a different world.

It's easy for us to see that sort of thing, grab a handful of Doritos, and think, *Wow, that sure looks weird.* But I have no doubt that for those tribal elders sitting around discussing the bride price, it's perfectly normal. Where they're from, that's the way things are done and probably have been done for as long as anyone can remember.

After all, it's their culture.

Perhaps you've had the experience firsthand of entering another culture. Many things in that culture you visited probably seem beautiful. Some aspects make no sense. And others probably seem completely upside down. But that cross-cultural experience of being taken out of your little corner of the world and being shown a different perspective can literally change your life, revealing where you're right on in your own culture…or where you're off track.

As we mentioned earlier, one of the reasons we need God's word is to help us get outside of ourselves to see the world through God's eyes—to see His truth rather than our distortions of it. You see, by ourselves we can easily get swept up in our own culture simply because it's what we're immersed in. We so easily start doing what we see others doing, saying what others are saying, and making decisions based on how others would make those same decisions. It's certainly difficult to follow Christ when we are staring down at the heels of everyone else around us.

But when we raise our eyes to meet God's gaze, seeing over the heads of everyone around us to His principles in Scripture, we are able to see beyond our culture, beyond our own short-sighted ways.

Time Will Tell.

//   How can time help us overcome cultural expectations?   //

Our culture often confuses chemistry with intimacy, telling us that intimacy happens simply by magnetic attraction. All you have to do is find the right person and bonding will happen as easily as two people in Velcro suits running into each other. But true intimacy, getting to know someone inside out, takes time.

Lots of time.

Psychologist Dr. Dorothy Tennov has studied the experience of what we call being "in love," and has found that rather than lasting a lifetime, as we'd like to believe, the romantic feeling lasts only about two years on average.[3] When your heart is pounding, however, it's easy to be persuaded by your culture expectations that those emotions are forever! But as you get to know each other over different seasons, you'll begin to see through that other person's veneer to the true grain of his or her personality. Therefore, if you have dated for more than two years, the veneer is just starting to rub off. Although the romance may be fading, it is at this point that commitment is truly challenged.

It's important, then, for the two of you to reveal yourselves through all seasons, for time will help take you from the fantasy of the "in love" experience to the reality of truly loving.

And *that* takes time.

Tried & Tested.

> // As cultural expectations continue to press on me, am I growing stronger or weaker in my "yes" to God? //

At the time, Abram and Sarai may have felt they were taking a step in faithfulness to God by having Abram produce a child through Sarai's maidservant. But interestingly, the Old Testament writer uses words here that mirror those in Genesis at the Fall: *Sarai…took…gave…to her husband.*[4]

Which sounds an awful lot like *Eve…took…gave…to her husband.*[5]

---

3   Chapman, Gary. *The Five Love Languages: How to Express Heartfelt Commitment to Your Mate.* (Chicago: Northfield Publishing, 2004): 30-31.
4   Waltke, Bruce. *Genesis.* (Grand Rapids: Zondervan, 2001): 252.
5   Genesis 3:6

In other words, the writer of Genesis is telling us, it's sin all over again. The same theme in a new key. In trying to be "faithful" to what God had promised, Abram took matters into his own hand, failing to trust God for how it would come about.

As we mentioned earlier, we tend to think of sin as doing "bad things," but it's more than that. Instead, as one writer put it, the psycho is at the door | p.034

> Saint Paul contrasts faith with sin when he says, "Whatever is not of faith is sin…." We usually think of sin as the opposite of virtue, and faith as the opposite of doubt. But virtue is a moral term, and doubt is an intellectual term. The opposite of moral virtue is moral vice, and the opposite of intellectual doubt is intellectual belief. Faith is deeper than either moral virtue or intellectual belief. Sin is deeper than either moral vice or intellectual doubt. Faith is a fundamental Yes to God with the center of our being, and sin—the state of sin as distinct from particular acts of sin—is the fundamental No to God with the center of our being. Faith is the opposite of sin. Faith is to sin what light is to darkness.[6]

God had a destiny for Abram's life—to be the father of many nations—but it wasn't just the destination that God was interested in. Abram's journey of faith— the waiting, the testing, the refining of his character—were *all* important to God. Abram, on the other hand, became so focused on fulfilling the promise, on seeing God's plan come about, that he tried to make things happen himself. As a result, he mixed up one of the most important details between here and there:

Saying *yes* to culture versus saying *yes* to God.

Abraham isn't faithful because he was somehow born with an extraordinary faith; he's faithful because he learned faith through his failings. He learned to see God as a result of the times he didn't see Him. When he's ultimately told by God to sacrifice his son—the very son he waited forever to have—he trusts God. He makes the preparations. And he almost goes through with the plan…but as we know, God

---

6   Kreeft, Peter. *Fundamentals of the Faith: Essays in Christian Apologetics*. (San Francisco: Ignatius Press, 1988): 171.

shows up and does the unexpected. God stops the sacrifice and provides a ram instead.

It's a wild story, and whatever questions it raises, it provides these answers: Faith involves radical obedience, and even when life seems out of control, God is in control.

God probably hasn't audibly told you who to marry, the way He talked to Abram. But that doesn't mean that He isn't speaking to you regarding your relationship. So ask yourself, *am I connecting all the dots between here and there myself, looking to cultural expectations of what makes a good mate?*

> *Or am I looking to God for direction in asking the right questions, and trusting Him in time for the right answers?*

So Jesus spoke to them: "You are masters at making yourselves look good in front of others, but God knows what's behind the appearance.

What society sees and calls monumental, God sees through and calls monstrous."

-Luke 16:15 (*The Message*)

I confess...
>   I like control.
>   I really do know what is best for me.
>   I like my list...it is mine...I have made it, and I like it.
>   I want.
>   I need.
>   I, I, I...

I guess my expectations are in me (and my list).

Oh, God help me to get real.
>   Help me to realize you are my God
>   and truly know what is best.

I confess YOU are in control.

Now that you are at the end of this section, take time to reflect on whether your expectations are realistic in regards to your future relationship. Gaining insight from those who have been there is always helpful. Go to your favorite coffee shop with a recently married couple. Informally chat with them about their adjustment to married life.

Listen specifically for some of their realistic and unrealistic expectations as they prepared to live life together. What are some false expectations regarding relationships have you observed in our culture? How can you tell the difference between a false expectation and reality? What are some false expectations you feel your partner has regarding your relationship? How can you as a couple work through any unrealistic expectations you have?

consider the_expectations

s_four

section_04
consider the boundaries

011 do I guard my heart or give my heart away?

....

When upperclassmen Mac and his friend Jack[1] were moving freshman into the residence hall he took a *huge* risk and stopped one sweet, young freshman whose cute smile caught his attention. After a brief conversation, it was all he could do to keep his mind on moving the rest of the girls into their rooms. Taking another risk, Mac and Jack called her and one of her friends to go out. Later Jack moved in on Mac and asked her out.

But she said…"*No!*"

Thinking on his feet Jack said, "Well, if you won't go out with me, will you go out with my roommate, Mac?"

She did and the rest is history. Mac's big risk of stopping Carolyn on the steps paid off. (Or was it Jack's risk of calling to ask her out? Or maybe Carolyn's risk of saying *no*, then *yes*?) All I know is that today my (Byron's) parents have been married fifty-six years. I agree with my dad, *it was worth the risk!*

The moment any relationship begins, there is risk. Every time a guy asks a gal out, every time a couple is wed, every time one person begins to love another, risk is right there ready to crash the party. As the relationship grows, risk grows, and the more there is to gain from the possibility of the relationship moving forward or to lose from getting hurt.

In relationships, there is no way around risk.

....
1   Those are their real names. I could never make up that "Mac and Jack" part and keep a straight face.

With great risk, however, comes the wonderful possibility of great reward:[2] Deep, intimate love. Unconditional acceptance. A unity unlike any found in any other human relationship on the face of this planet. It isn't easy to navigate the emotional boundaries between these poles of risk and reward, however. The lines are always shifting. As trust grows, we wonder whether it's okay to open ourselves more fully. As we are hurt or doubt or fear, we withdraw or shut ourselves down. And in this dance back and forth, some people guard their hearts too much, protecting them when more risk would be healthy. Others give their hearts away too much, too early, risking indiscriminately.

Can we find a balance?

How do we answer the question, *do I guard my heart or give my heart away?*

You Can't Eliminate Emotional Risk, But You Can Lessen It.

//   I can't eliminate emotional risk in a relationship,
so how can I handle it?   //

Our unmet emotional needs are powerful motivators toward fear or longing, and sometimes we look past God's purposes to meet those needs outside of His provision. Like a raging river, our needs form strong currents capable of sweeping us into decisions we never thought we'd make. Such as marrying someone we never should have. Or in my mom and dad's case, nearly missing out on a wonderful relationship because they were too afraid to call.

Marriage and family author and speaker Dr. John Van Epp has written a book called *How to Avoid Marrying a Jerk,*[3] in which he discusses a healthy process of growing in

---

2   As crude an analogy as it may be, a relationship is similar to financial investing. When you're first starting out, you don't have much money, so you can't invest much and the risk is relatively low. Likewise, when you very first begin a relationship, you haven't invested much emotionally. But after time together, after sharing your heart and allowing that other person to see you for who you really are, your relationship has more emotional or relational "capital." You have "invested" your time, your energy, and your very heart.

3   Van Epp, John. *How to Avoid Marrying a Jerk: The Foolproof Way to Follow Your Heart Without Losing Your Mind.* (New York: McGraw Hill, 2007).

intimacy. He outlines five components that should be experienced in succession, each one necessary before moving to the next:

Know ➲ Trust ➲ Rely ➲ Commit ➲ Sex

Simply put, you can't trust someone that you don't first know. Likewise, you can't rely on someone that you don't trust. You don't commit to someone that you can't rely on. And you shouldn't have sex with someone that you haven't committed to in a marital covenant.

You can't rush this progression; to move through these stages, you must have time. It takes time to trust someone. It takes time to know that you can rely on them. It takes time to emotionally take that step of commitment into the marriage covenant, which then expresses itself sexually.[4]

Following this process doesn't eliminate risk, of course. In spite of the title of Dr. Van Epp's wonderful book, there's no foolproof, 100% guaranteed way to avoid marrying someone who won't *become* a jerk. There's both real beauty and real danger in our free will. You can follow each one of those steps faithfully and still wind up getting hurt. But by following those principles for healthy attachment, you minimize the risk greatly.

For a seriously dating couple, it's a difficult dance. If you feel tension trying to navigate those components, join the millions of other couples on *that* dance floor! Still, they provide a helpful matrix through which to make decisions when one person may want to take further steps and the other may want to slow down. They can also help provide guidance if one of you reacts to emotional boundaries by shutting off from the risk (and relationship), kissing intimacy good-bye.

Are You Kissing Intimacy Good-bye? (Over-spiritualizing Relationships)

//   Am I hiding any insecurity by being hyper-spiritual?   //

------

4   You could even go one step further and say it takes time after marriage to figure out *sex*!

I (Carla) had known Byron for a while during our dating relationship, but I kept him at arm's length. It was wonderful to have him in my *life*, but even after I'd grown to trust him, I wasn't really letting him into my heart. By not letting him in, I thought I was being strong; in reality, I was being weak.

Why?

At the time, I was over-spiritualizing a lot of things in my life to the point where I thought I didn't really need *anybody*—that God and God alone would meet *all* my needs. I believed I was guarding my heart, when instead I was guarding my insecurities. My over-spiritualizing was an attempt to conceal inner pride, while on the outside I tried to appear spiritually heroic, getting recognition for the Bible studies I was leading and the women I was discipling. As long as my relationships were in *my* control, I was okay.

What's wrong with believing that God meets your needs? you may think. *Isn't that part of what you've been trying to tell us in this book? That we're complete in Christ?*

God doesn't meet *all* our emotional needs directly. It's true that He *could* meet them head-on if He wanted to. But the remarkable thing is that He doesn't. He's like a parent working on a project around the home who wants to let his kids join in so they can learn. Our growth and maturity is more important to God than getting the job done "right," because for God the job is often more about our growth. So while I am complete in Christ in terms of His work of salvation, Christ invites others around me to join Him in that other part of His work—my sanctification.

a life lab for our spiritual growth | p.036

People afraid to let go of control and risk emotionally and relationally often cling to all sorts of things: relationships, possessions, their image in the eyes of those around them—even clinging immaturely to God in hopes He'll spoon-feed them the easy life. Over-spiritualizing life and dating relationships, hiding behind a spiritual façade and spiritual lingo, is often a mask for insecurity or pain. It can be a path of less resistance, and those who take this path can be like children afraid to leave home for fear of the responsibility. But God wants us to risk in healthy ways—respecting His boundaries, of course—but not shying away from appropriate, mature interaction.

We've known couples, for example, who have waited to kiss until the altar. It's *great* that those couples value purity—and we're certainly not saying you necessarily *should* kiss before the altar. That's your choice. However, just beware that if you *are* over-spiritualizing the decision you are not hiding any emotional and relational insecurities. Many of the couples we have known who did the ol' "*wait until the alter deal*" regret it, because when over-spiritualizing our actions becomes a way of avoiding appropriate expressions of love, we can circumvent the body of Christ's powerful influence in one another's lives, bonding doesn't take place, and intimacy remains at arm's length.

Over-spiritualizing is certainly an effective way to remain safe.

To keep the relationship under control (our control).

To maintain appearances.

But then, that isn't really the point of healthy, appropriate intimacy, is it?

Emotional Intimacy: Out of Order.

//   What are some of the ways we get our emotional
boundaries out of order?   //

While some deny their emotional needs and revert to over-spiritualizing to hide their insecurity, others look to human relationships for what only God can give us: ultimate significance, security, and belonging. People with strong emotional needs often throw themselves into relationships to find what they feel they're lacking inside. Neither approach is healthy. And so as you assess emotional boundaries in your relationship—whether to open your heart further or protect it—you must assess your own neediness.

In their book, *Intimate Encounters*, marriage and family ministers Dr. David & Teresa Ferguson discuss areas helpful in nurturing intimacy in a healthy way:

Affectionate Caring - "I care about you."
→ Vulnerable Communication - "I trust you."
→ Joint Accomplishment - "I need you."
→ Mutual Giving - "I love you."[5]

Note the movement from care to trust to need to love. The insecure, over-spiritual person will often move from care to need to love—bypassing trust. The emotionally needy, over-relational person will often jump straight to need. And our culture often begins at love and works backward: I love you and need you; therefore, I will trust you and perhaps care for you if you meet my needs. Therefore, like Dr. Van Epp's components of relationship attachment, a healthy progression through these emotional components can help.

Doing this will allow intimacy to be nurtured in healthy ways in your relationships, helping you avoid emotional detachment or possibly over-attachment.

Anticipate Your Emotional Neediness Before You "Bonk."

//   How can I assess whether either of us is overly emotionally needy or not? If one of us is, what can we do about it?   //

If you haven't already figured it out from what Byron has said, I (Carla) love to run. I love getting outside and moving. I love pushing my body. And I love the feeling that comes after a good workout.

But I can only run if I take care of my body.

If you're an athlete, perhaps you know what it's like to "bonk." Bonking occurs during intense exercise when glycogen stored in the body runs out. Go too long

---

5   Ferguson, Dr. David & Teresa & Thurman, Dr. Chris & Holly. *The Pursuit of Intimacy Leader's Guide* (Nashville: Thomas Nelson Publishers, 1993): 48.

without refueling and you can start feeling dizzy and even have trouble standing up. And if an athlete waits until she feels this way, it's already too late.

You have to anticipate your physical need before it gets you in trouble.

The same applies to our emotional needs. It's difficult for people to see their own emotional neediness, but if you can recognize it, be open with your partner. Have an honest conversation, asking for what you need, and you'll probably earn some respect.

Then, if you do sense neediness in yourself, or if someone you trust has pointed it out, ask yourself, *why? Why am I needy? Is it because of family patterns I experienced growing up, because of unspoken messages from parents? Is it because of wounds from previous relationships?* This is important because failure to address these questions will affect your capacity to move forward.

When I see that Byron is needy, it is so important to address this in a positive manner. I have to remind myself to keep Byron's best interests in mind. If I want him to change in a certain way with a selfish motive in mind, he will sense that every time. A good question to ask myself is, *am I providing a safe place for my partner to talk about a very vulnerable subject?*

These all are much easier to address, of course, if you both have a firm foundation in God. Many couples tell us that God is part of their relationship, but in reality He's more of a spectator on the sidelines watching the game being played than a participant calling the plays in the huddle.

Keep in mind that when our identity hinges on what others think of us or when we try to find in other people what only Christ can give us, we will be disappointed every time. But an unmoving foundation in Christ allows you to risk in your human relationships without being leveled when it does not work out...or when you find out she said *no* to Jack and *yes* to you.

If you feel tension navigating these emotional boundaries of your relationship, that's alright. It's okay to be in that place, because that tension is a natural part of the process of moving closer together.

Stanley Mac and his bride of 50+ years, my (Byron's) dad and mom, have found that joy and closeness don't just come from *wishing*.

They come from being together through the good and bad,

from proving your love over and over,

from developing a bond of trust

and going the extra mile to help meet needs.

Carla and I—just like my Mom and Dad—go through cycles of knowing and not knowing how to move within this emotional dance. As you do, remember that time has a great deal to do with how you navigate your emotional boundaries, with how much you step forward or back.

We didn't say it would be an easy dance. But it's a good dance.

Very good.

Just ask my mom—she knows everything!

012 what do I do with this sex-driven life?

....

When Carla and I got married, the first gift we received was a Bassett hound puppy.

At first I wasn't sure what I thought about the idea of being a dog owner. But then, as I saw how much joy it gave Carla, I began to soften. *How hard could it be to own a Bassett hound?* I thought. I mean, a slobbering, 180-pound St. Bernard or even a hyper, high-maintenance Pomeranian is one thing, but Bassett hounds just lie around all day on the porch. Their droopy faces make them look like they just woke up from a two-year nap. They'd trip over their ears if they ran. *What was there to worry about?*

So we kept Benson in our little house on the Central Texas prairie.

As we soon found out, however, Benson was no ordinary Bassett hound. Somewhere in his past, he must have been laid on a table in Dr. Frankenstein's laboratory and given the energy of a greyhound, a severe case of ADHD, and the sexual drive of a dog perpetually in heat. Every night when we'd let Benson out of the house, you could hear him tearing off into the night, whooping it up. He was like a drunken college student for whom every night was spring break in Cancun as he ran around driven by his nose and his penis. To this day, probably half of the dogs in that town have Bassett hound blood in them.

Us youth ministers were housing a playboy dog.

When I tell that story to young singles, I can just see them imagining Benson running around the neighborhood, carousing with other dogs. Many of them may imagine him going at it with the female poodles and think, *"You go, Benson! You're the man!"*

Unlike us, Benson acted purely by his senses. If he wanted to do it, he did it. If it felt good, he did it again and again. It's true that we have those same urges, those same animalistic desires. But the difference between us and Benson (well, thankfully there are many differences between us and Benson) is that as humans we have God's image upon us. That is, there are traits that we share with God—in some ways we are "God-like." For those who follow Christ, we also have God's Spirit within us. And though we sometimes act in ways that are more Benson-like than Christ-like, the fact that we are made in God's image should make a profound difference in the way we conduct ourselves.

We are a fundamentally different kind of creature.

The Wrong Question.

// Is *"How far can we go?"* a good question to ask? //

Byron and I sometimes talk with couples who are struggling physically. Basically, they are asking, "Is it alright to experiment sexually? Since we *think* we are going to get married, what is acceptable and unacceptable behavior in this area? After all, how can you buy the car if you don't test drive the engine?" By this they mean, how far can we go physically in our relationship without destroying it? Where can we put our hands and not put our hands? If sexual activity is a continuum, how far can we slide toward sexual intercourse before God starts shaking His head *no*?

On the surface, that may seem like a great question, and you're certainly right to be concerned about what God thinks. But to put it rather bluntly, *isn't that question asking, how much can I get away with? How close to the line can I walk before it's sin?*

marriage is no "get out of jail free" pass | p.04

And is that really the right question to be asking?

But it's an expression of our love, you might reply.

Well, *yes* and *no*. Those sexual feelings you have toward each other are normal. They are very real. They represent a wonderful attraction between the two of you. But here is the deal. During this season prior to marriage, you are going through strict training to understand real love. Trust us, the process will make you stronger and a better lover after marriage. And this testing of your sexual attraction will deepen or destroy your *true* love for each other.[1] You may feel that your physical relationship is an expression of your love, but if you are stepping over physical boundaries, then it's an expression of your desire. Of your attraction. Of your lust even. But not your love.

If you really want to love, rather than asking how far you can go *with* your partner, what about asking how far you can go *for* your partner? Rather than asking what God will permit you to do with your desire, what about asking what God would most desire you to do? Instead of asking, *how far can we go?*, what about asking, *how far I can go for my partner? For my God?*

Learn to be a real love-maker.   can you say "I love you," no strings attached? | p.141

That's an effort God will honor.

Sex, Self-Control, & Sanctification.

//   How are sex, self-control, and sanctification connected?   //

The truth is, sex isn't just about the sex. Our sexuality is connected to our spirituality, an intimate connection between our spirits and our genitals. If we live as if sex is primarily about skin on skin, we miss far deeper realities. And if we look at sex as expressing our "love" for each other outside the covenant of marriage, we miss the point entirely.

----

1   Once you "know that you know," we recommend that you don't have a year-long engagement (or longer), because it puts you in difficult situations physically that were never intended for couples in their 20's and 30's.

The apostle Paul touched on this when he wrote,

> *It is God's will that you should be sanctified; that you should avoid sexual immorality; that each of you should learn to control his own body in a way that is holy and honorable, not in passionate lust like the heathen, who do not know God; and that in this matter no one should wrong his brother or take advantage of him. The Lord will punish men for all such sins, as we have already told you and warned you. For God did not call us to be impure, but to live a holy life. Therefore, he who rejects this instruction does not reject man but God, who gives you his Holy Spirit.*[2]

Did you catch that?

Paul uses *sex* and *sanctification* in the same sentence. He not only relates avoiding sexual immorality with God's work of sanctification; he suggests a lack of sexual self-control is characteristic of those who don't know God.

Ouch.

In other words, God is saying through His word, *the more you know me and my kind of love, the more I will help you be able to exercise self control.*

Part of being a great lover—which includes having a great sex life in marriage—is preparing to be self-controlled sexually. When you're self-controlled in your faithfulness to your partner, your love mirrors that of Christ.

But you can't do it alone. You may be able to "control your own body" by yourself for a time, but eventually you'll struggle. It's no wonder, then, that *discipline* and *disciple* both come from the same root word. *Disciple* means to be a learner, one who follows another's example, and so if we are disciples of Christ, *disciplining* ourselves doesn't simply mean turning from the bad; it also means following the good.

---

2   1 Thessalonians 4:3-8

Do you have a greater desire to prepare for God's liberating best than your great, immediate desire for physical intimacy?

That's an important question to answer because by disciplining yourself, following the leading and grace of God's Spirit, you'll better be able to resist Satan, who wants nothing more than to lead you astray.

Destroyed or Deepened?

> // If it were up to you, how would you go about destroying relationships? //

The apostle John tells us that "the thief comes only to steal and kill and destroy,"[3] and by "thief" he's not talking about some guy who wants your money.

He's talking about someone who wants your *soul.*

Satan.

If you were setting out to steal, kill, and destroy a generation—as Satan is—why *not* use sex? It's attractive. It's pleasurable. It's quick. It's easily within reach. And because sexual intimacy superglues hearts together, it is incredibly difficult and painful to separate a couple after intercourse without emotional and spiritual fallout (even Hollywood agrees with that). Satan no doubt takes a perverse pleasure in twisting one of God's most beautiful, most constructive creations into something destructive. If you wanted to harm God's creation, you could accomplish all three goals in one premature sexual act:

Killing.

Stealing.

---

3   John 10:10

Destroying.

God's law doesn't exist to squelch our fun; it's there to protect us from precisely this kind of harm. And as the apostle Paul says about the call to purity and living a holy life, "he who rejects this instruction does not reject man but God, who gives you his Holy Spirit."[4] And "rejecting this instruction" leads to severe consequences.

Joe and Dee know about that all too well.

The two of them were Christ followers who desired God's best for their lives. They started dating their freshman year in college, and right from the beginning they spent a lot of time praying together. They shared everything about themselves, talked about their dreams, laughed, and genuinely enjoyed being together. But, ironically, the more time they spent praying, the more difficult it was to control their physical urges.

After six months, they began crossing boundaries they never thought they would. As we all hear so often, nothing felt wrong at the time. Their physical relationship began to overpower all other areas of their relationship and after several months of sexual intercourse, Dee became pregnant. *Do we have an abortion?* they wondered. *Do we get married and keep the baby? Do we have the baby and give it up for adoption?* But beyond those questions, they kept asking themselves, *why did this happen? How could we have avoided this painful experience?* But it was too late for anything but hindsight. Now, how could they put the pieces back together?

The two decided to get married. They had a beautiful child and appeared to be doing all the right things as they journeyed through life. After a second child and eight years of marriage, however, Dee began to struggle. She was still searching for who she was, looking for purpose and meaning, always wanting more out of life and her relationship with Joe. She felt isolated and alienated…then attracted to another man.

And began an affair. Same song, different verse.

---

4   I Thessalonians 4:8

Joe found out, of course.

The ramifications of Dee's sexual misbehavior continued to haunt them as they filed for divorce. They never intended to lead such a painful life, but their inability to control their physical desires destroyed their relationship and caused great emotional and spiritual pain, not only to themselves, but to their entire family—and especially their children. *But it could never happen to us*, they believed.

Or so they thought.

You hear stories like this all the time—stories often meant to make you feel "you better behave or else"—so it's easy to sort of shrug off the message. But it happened to them. It happens to countless others.

Why couldn't it happen to you?

More to the point, what are you doing so that it *won't* it happen to you?

Sex is a sacred act, consecrated by God for the intimate expression of the marital relationship. But the most beautiful of acts can turn ugly when Satan gets his hands on it. When you're seriously dating, it's easy to assume that when you're married, all your sexual issues will disappear. But being able to have sex in marriage doesn't make those issues go away. Therefore, having sex *before* marriage side-steps the issues you're facing, burying them now to resurface later. Your physical body may not know the difference between being married and unmarried, but your mind and emotions know. That tension between the two exposes your deep need for intimacy with God during this time. It's all part of your spiritual formation.

The apostle Peter encouraged men and women "to abstain from sinful desires, which war against your soul."[5] Unfortunately, the souls of men and women *are* destroyed in body, mind, and spirit when sexual intimacy is expressed outside marriage. As you grasp this part of Satan's big-picture strategy, however, it can begin to lose its power over you. It's like peeking at the enemy battle plans laid out on a table and seeing what's coming at you.

----

5   1 Peter 2:11

You can anticipate.

Prepare.

Be on the alert.

Ready.

What Are You Reflecting?

// What kind of life are my physical boundaries reflecting? //

If sex isn't just about sex—and if how you handle your sexual desires and pressures prior to marriage mirrors your spiritual relationship with God—*what then are you reflecting?*

Lust? A desire to have now what isn't yours?

Impatience? Rushing ahead instead of holding off for better?

Faithlessness? Not trusting in God and what lies unseen ahead of you?

Or *love*? Patient. Protecting. Hoping. Persevering.

You see, sexuality that reflects and honors God is one of the most powerful sermons one will ever preach. For seriously dating couples, the struggle to remain pure is a constant and vivid reminder of one's present spiritual longing. Remaining pure for marriage here on earth is a reflection of remaining pure for that union with Christ that one day will come. For someday, when Christ returns, all that marriage is about will be revealed in a moment of piercing joy at Jesus' return, a party the likes of which this universe has never seen. And we, the Church, are the bride of Christ waiting for that wedding feast to begin.

So think of this from God's perspective: Would you want to be united in oneness with someone who flirts with other lovers? Someone who doesn't give a rip what you say? You see, sexual purity doesn't just reflect and affect your relationship with your partner. It also reveals what kind of a relationship you have with your God.[6]

As the faith-filled lives of Abraham, Abel, Enoch, and Noah are being described, the author of the book of Hebrews writes an interesting thing in response to their patient vision for the good that is to come: "Therefore God is not ashamed to be called their God."

God was *not ashamed to be called their God.*

May that be said of us all—by our words, by our actions, by our sexuality—that God is unashamed to be called our God. That instead, when we are united with Him forever, He will be as ecstatic and emotional as a groom on his wedding day.

We can be driven by a higher calling.

Not by our nose and penis like ol' Benson.

---

6   Hebrews 11:16

013 can you say "I love you," no strings attached?

....

The big three! I never tire of hearing three words: *I love you*.

A few weeks after I first said those "Big Three" to Carla, she found herself in the ER after a physical education class on softball fast pitch mechanics. A big 6'5" muscle-head had let a wild pitch go that caught Carla unaware and smashed her jaw.

As she was recovering in the hospital after surgery, I brought her a blender, flowers, and recipes for how to eat for six weeks with her mouth wired shut. You see, as a sophomore in high school, I broke my jaw playing football when I took a helmet under my facemask. It was during those daily hospital visits with Carla that I finally captured her heart.

I think it was the blender, but I am not sure.

One night after visiting hours were over (she did not want me to leave), she looked me in the eye and mumbled, "I love you!" At least that's what it sounded like because her mouth was horribly bruised and wired shut.

"What?" I said. "I can't hear you."

She gave me a sweet, knowing look and mumbled, "You know what I said."

Acting as if I could not hear her (really I just wanted her to say it over and over again), I kept asking, *what?* She would mumble it again and again until she finally wrote on paper, "ILY!"

My heart still pounds as I write these words. I can't hear them enough.

I LOVE YOU!

I really think it was the blender that did it.

Are there any more powerful words than "*I love you*"? Those three little words express in big ways the deepest virtue a human is possible of, but they can also be used in powerfully manipulative ways. Sometimes when we say "I love you" we attach conditions without even knowing it. We may say "I love you" without realizing we're saying it to get something in return. We may say "I love you" because we feel valued and want to keep the good feelings flowing. We "love," but often with all kinds of strings attached.

But love is not a currency for getting what we want.

Love is not manipulation.

Love is freely given, without expectation of anything in return.

And we all have a long way to go in understanding and living that kind of love.

A love with strings attached is based on how the other person measures up to our expectations; a love without strings attached is based on loving the person just as they are. But it takes real wisdom to know when to step into a relationship marked by unconditional love, in which you can say "I love you," *no strings attached*.

There is a progression that my buddy P-Dodd declares starts with the BIG THREE (I love you!), then moves to the BIG FOUR (Will you marry me?), followed by the BIG FIVE (Can we have sex tonight?), and somehow works its way around to the BIG SIX (Why are you so stinkin' moody?).

Love is Kind, Compassionate, and Forgiving.

// What does it mean to be kind, compassionate,
and forgiving to my partner? //

Among the Jewish rabbis of Jesus' day, forgiving a brother up to four times was the norm.[1] So when Peter said to Jesus, "How many times shall I forgive my brother when he sins against me? Up to seven times?"[2] he may have been trying to out-do the tradition of their day. Kind of like saying, *Hey, if forgiving four times is really being forgiving, what if we bump that up a bit for good measure?* It's as if Peter was trying to impress Jesus with an over-the-top approach to forgiveness.

Jesus, of course, isn't interested in out-doing the standard to look good, nor in rules for rules' sake. He's interested in a change of heart and seeing relationships brought back to their original intent, and so he undercuts the disciples' expectations. Peter's suggestion may have sounded impressive to everyone else, but Jesus had a different idea.

No, not seven times, he replies. *Seventy times seven.*

In other words, he's saying, don't limit yourself, because you'll have to extend forgiveness again and again in your relationships. Don't limit your forgiveness, because people need all the grace they can get.

Fast forward a few decades. With the hindsight of Christ's sacrificial death, the apostle Paul wrote to his fellow believers at Ephesus, "Be kind and compassionate to one another, forgiving each other, just as in Christ God forgave you."[3] It's a beautiful image not only because it gives us a glimpse of how we are to treat one another; it's beautiful because it reminds us how the Heavenly Father has treated us.

Kindly.

---

1   Hill, David. *The Gospel of Matthew: The New Century Bible Commentary* (Grand Rapids: William B. Eerdmans Publishing Company, reprinted 1996): 277.
2   Matthew 18:21
3   Ephesians 4:32

Compassionately.

Forgiving again…and again…and again.

And if that's what we need from God, it's certainly what we need from one another.

Love Builds Each Other Up.

// What does it mean to build my partner up? //

When I married Carla, I knew she was a rock, and as I watched her interact with others around her, I also suspected that she would make a great mother. But, boy, I had no idea what a high degree of integrity she has and what an incredible mother she would become! After nearly twenty-five years of marriage, raising three children together, and partnering in ministry with her, I've really seen Carla in action.

And, can you believe it, I get to love her like no other human on this planet gets to do. I have the opportunity to grow into the world's foremost expert on Carla. Anyone who marries becomes a lifelong student of their spouse, and God uses these intimate "studies in love" to help shape each another for His Kingdom.

Different buildings have different ways of being built up—you are crazy to use a welding torch to build an igloo or log cabin. Likewise, we all have different ways of being built up, of receiving love. As Gary Chapman points out in his book *The Five Love Languages: How to Express Heartfelt Commitment to Your Mate*, some of us feel loved most when we're shown physical affection. Some of us respond to words of encouragement; others respond best to quality time together or to acts of service. And for some, tangible gifts that show the other person was thinking of us are what touch our hearts most.

Because we're all different, we're all going to experience love differently.

That takes effort, because the ways of love that come naturally to me aren't necessarily the ways that Carla best receives love. But the apostle Paul nudges us toward each other's love languages when he wrote, "Be imitators of God, therefore, as dearly loved children and live a life of love, just as Christ loved us and gave himself up for us as a fragrant offering and sacrifice to God."[4]   Living that "life of love" as Christ offered and sacrificed Himself is a lifelong process. And by building up your partner—loving in ways you aren't accustomed to and giving yourself sacrificially—you're not only building up your partner.

You're building God's Kingdom.

Love is Learning to Submit to Each Other.

//   What does it mean to submit to each other?   //

Later in that letter to the church at Ephesus, the apostle Paul wrote, "Submit to one another out of reverence for Christ."[5] The word we translate "reverence" comes from the Greek word *phobos*. There's a related word you may be more familiar with: *phobia*. A "fear of." Another translation captures this nuance when it puts the verse this way: *"Be subject to one another in the fear of Christ."* (NASB).

But the fear that this verse speaks of is different from any of the phobias that we're familiar with: *claustrophobia*, a fear of closed in places. *Anuptaphobia*, fear of staying single. Or *gamophobia*, fear of marriage. Or my fear, *ophidiophobia*, a fear of snakes. Instead, the fear that this verse speaks of is based on reverence, which is the key to submission. One definition of *reverence* is "to stand in awe of," and it is our reverence that allows us to submit, that turns forced obligation into voluntary participation.

That "voluntarily" part is crucial. Our staff absolutely loves it when people ask whether they can volunteer to help with our ministry. Can they *help*? Are you kidding?! *Can they ever.* We love that request because however much skill they

---

4   Ephesians 5:1-2
5   Ephesians 5:21

bring, volunteers come with one of the most important ingredients for ministry, one that can't be taught: *a willing, enthusiastic heart*. Submission, in fact, could be defined as "voluntarily cooperating with one another out of love for God and love for one another."

But notice, it is our reverence for *Christ*, not for our *partner*, that Scripture points to. It is that reverence for Him that creates our voluntary submission for our partner. That is, if we are disciples of Christ, following in His footsteps, we submit because Christ Himself submitted, even to death on the cross.

When we submit to one other, building each other up, we become more than the sum of our parts. Think of players on a football team. One may get more attention than the others, but that player in the spotlight is not more important than the others. An incredible running back without a good offensive line will have a difficult time getting past the line of scrimmage. A great quarterback without a receiver with good hands suddenly finds himself mediocre at best.

What is true in our relationships on the field and with others is especially true in that most intimate of relationships—marriage. Because there the two may become one, but the two add up to more than just the sum of their parts. In marriage, one plus one not only equals a unified *one*; one plus one also equals far more than two in the powerful effect that married couple can have on those around them.

You may not be asked to physically sacrifice your life for your spouse, but we'd be lying to you if we said that you won't have to die to self, as the apostle Paul put it. And dying is…well, painful. It is as if you are lowering a casket with your comfortable but selfish ways into the ground. But keep in mind that selfless, Godly love is what helps us take steps of faith into a deeper relationship, moving into new territory.

Through your uncertainties.

    Into the unknowns.

        Being able to truly say "*I love you*."

No strings attached.

It *is* worth dying for!

Loving God, No Strings Attached.

//   What does it mean to love God, no strings attached?   //

For the ancient Israelites, the great stories of God's work in their ancestors' lives—the story of Creation, the Flood, and the enslavement in Egypt and the Exodus—would have all been told and retold as beloved classics.

But there's another story—an unlikely story—that was told over and over as well.

The story of Rahab the prostitute.

It is certainly one of the most dramatic conversion stories in Scripture, and you can just imagine the scene leading up to her turn-around: murmurs among the people of Jericho of how the Israelites were advancing in the land. Widespread fear. And perhaps because of those whispered conversations, Rahab heard what God was doing and the seeds of her belief were planted.

Somewhere among the stories being told around Jericho, faith began to grow in her.

When the Israelite spies came to Jericho, the king of Jericho found out about their intent and sent to Rahab for them, where they were housed. But she did an unexpected thing. Rather than turn them over to her own king, she covered for them. She gave her king the old "they went that way" line and then talked with the spies. And at some point during that tense, secretive evening, she took the risk and revealed her growing faith.

The spies agreed to spare Rahab's life and the lives of her family members—her father, mother, brother, sisters, and "all who belong to them."[6] The spies' only condition was that she must tie a scarlet cord from the same window they escape through so that the Israelite army can spare her when they return. If she attached the string, then she and her family would be spared.

So Rahab took the step, tied the string, and left her old life behind.

This story, Rahab's story—the story of the foreign-born, godless prostitute turned to Yahweh—becomes a *classic* among the Israelite people. For Rahab to be featured among those faith-filled lives in the book of Hebrews[7] and one of four women in Matthew's genealogy,[8] her story must have been passed down through the generations. Had she *not* chosen to follow Yahweh as her God and live obediently, the likelihood of her being mentioned in Hebrews 11 would have been nonexistent.

What a story it was then! Even in her own culture in Jericho she was likely despised. But God didn't write her out of His redemptive story. For Rahab to be spoken as highly of as she was in both the Old and New Testaments, she must have had a remarkable turn-around in her life, becoming a woman of "healthy boundaries." Though Jesus hadn't yet spoken the words, she took the spirit of them to heart: *"If you love me, you will obey what I command."[9]*

Life for Rahab was never the same. She married Salmon and gave birth to Boaz. Boaz married Ruth, who ended up being the great grandmother of the powerful King David (and in the lineage of Jesus). Rahab's faithfulness—her new life of love to her God, new people, and family—led her to become one of three women mentioned among the Jewish heroes of the faith.

What a great story of forgiveness, compassion, and kindness. She didn't look back. In making the switch, Rahab's string attached to her window in Jericho led to a completely different life, a willing and enthusiastic heart for God—*no strings*

---

6   Joshua 2:12-13. Interestingly—but perhaps not so surprisingly—these verses never mention a husband of Rahab's.
7   Rahab is also mentioned in James 2:25.
8   Matthew 1:5
9   John 14:15

attached. "For the LORD your God is God in heaven above and on the earth below," she declared to the Israelite spies that night in Jericho. She left behind her past and looked ahead to the future, being able to say "I love you" unconditionally both to her new God and, later, to her new husband. Which made a way for love to build up future generations in a way that Rahab could have never imagined.

And the rest, as they say, is history.

God's history.

His story.

/ / / / / / / / / / / / /

This is how much God loved the world: He gave his Son, his one and only Son. And this is why: so that no one need be destroyed; by believing in him, anyone can have a whole and lasting life.

God didn't go to all the trouble of sending his Son merely to point an accusing finger, telling the world how bad it was. He came to help, to put the world right again. Anyone who trusts in him is acquitted; anyone who refuses to trust him has long since been under the death sentence without knowing it. And why? Because of that person's failure to believe in the one-of-a-kind Son of God when introduced to him.

This is the crisis we're in: God-light streamed into the world, but men and women everywhere ran for the darkness. They went for the darkness because they were not really interested in pleasing God. Everyone who makes a practice of doing evil, addicted to denial and illusion, hates God-light and won't come near it, fearing a painful exposure. But anyone working and living in truth and reality welcomes God-light so the work can be seen for the God-work it is.

-John 3:16-21 (*The Message*)

Now that you are at the end of this section, take time to reflect on the necessary boundaries that help frame a solid relationship. A trusted older friend/mentor once gave me (Byron) the "Consequences of a Moral Tumble" and encouraged me to put a copy in my desk at work. He challenged me that whenever I feel particularly vulnerable to sexual temptation, I should review what effects my action could have.

Consider the following:

- Grieving the Lord who redeemed me. Dragging His sacred name into the mud.
- One day having to look Jesus, the Righteous Judge, in the face and give an account of my actions.
- Inflicting untold hurt on my wife; my best friend and loyal wife.
- Causing shame to my family. Hurting my children whom I love so much.
- Creating a form of guilt that is awfully hard to shake. Even though God would forgive me, would I forgive myself?
- Possibly bearing the physical consequences of such diseases as gonorrhea, syphilis, chlamydia, herpes, and AIDS; perhaps infecting my wife or, in the case of AIDS, even causing her death.
- Possibly causing pregnancy, with the personal and financial implications, including a lifelong reminder of my sin.
- Bringing shame and hurt to fellow friends and co-workers.
- Invoking shame and life-long embarrassment upon myself.

section_05
consider the sacrifice
//////////////

014 why is commitment so difficult to commit to?

....

Commitment.

It's a word that makes many of us cringe. We often feel that it hems us in.

Cramps our style.

Causes us to give up things we want to hold tightly to.

If commitment is really as good as some people would have us believe, then why does it seem so constraining? Why is it that we sometimes need commitment wrung out of us? What is it about commitment that makes us avoid it?

Why is *commitment so difficult for us to commit to?*

Commitment's Easy. (It's Sacrifice That's Difficult.)

// What is it about commitment that makes it so difficult? //

Truth is, commitment really isn't so bad; you know people committed to all kinds of things. Following their favorite football team through to the playoffs. Diving back into that page-turner of a book. Spending weekend after weekend deer hunting. Or bass fishing. Or snow skiing. Sure, it's easy to find people committed to *those* things for obvious reasons.

Why then is commitment in our relationships so difficult to commit to?

Probably the main reason commitment is so difficult to commit to is that…well, to put it quite bluntly, we're so often selfish. It's difficult to focus on others when we want to focus on ourselves—or when we want others to focus on us.

That's simplifying matters, of course, because commitment is difficult for many reasons. Those who have been burned by relationships in the past will likely be more guarded when it comes to commitment. It's difficult to be vulnerable when you've been hurt by someone you love. Commitment is also difficult because of the unknowns that lie before you. *What if that other person really gets to know me and rejects me?*   into-me-see & "perfect love casts out fear…" | p.060 & 061

Faced with that kind of risky commitment—sacrifice—I (Carla) remember looking in the mirror and asking, *am I really ready to give up the fun of dating other guys in order to move forward with my relationship with Byron? Do I really want to change? Do I really want to let go of something that is fun? Do I really want to give up what I enjoy for the sake of Byron?* In other words, *do I really want to step deeper into the relationship?*

To ultimately commit until death do us part?

Roadblock Ahead: What's Stopping You from Sacrifice?

//   In what ways is it difficult for me to sacrifice for my partner?
What do my inner questions tell me about my hesitancy to commit?   //

On the surface, sacrifice often looks or feels like great loss, but with that loss paradoxically comes great gain. Forfeiting something valuable for something considered to have a greater value can sound so reasonable, so easy even. But we all know the truth.

What is it that is keeping you from taking that next step? If you have fears or uncertainties or concerns, what are they?

Your answer will be revealing, for it gives you a clue to what is holding you back from commitment, from sacrifice. You see, any uncertainties you may have are like roadblocks on a highway. If you were driving along and suddenly came across roadblocks, but didn't know what they were for, what would you do? They could be there because the road is washed out ahead, because a bridge is structurally unsound, or because the government is covering up a UFO landing site.[1] There are all kinds of reasons that roadblock could be there.

Your feelings—whether you would defend them before a Congressional hearing or not as worth acting upon—you feel for a reason. Listen to them. If you are worried about missing your regular weekend fishing trips with your friends more than you desire a covenant relationship with the woman who loves you, that reveals an important piece of information about your values and level of commitment. (Sure, you know you're not *supposed* to feel that way…but, well, *you do*.) In order to take that step into marriage, you will need to weigh them to see where your values truly lie. There are all kinds of fears that may be blocking your path: *Perhaps you're afraid you won't be treated well by the guy you're with. He may love you in so many ways, but still he acts pretty harshly in how he treats you. Or you may be wondering why she seems to still flirt with others. What does that mean?*

If questions like these keep entering your mind, recognize these as good roadblocks to have. You must face those uncertainties head-on. They are there, after all. But *why* are they there?

What is it that's stopping you from making the sacrifice?

----

1   Which happens all the time here in Texas. *Big* UFO's….

For *Which* Cause?

> //   For which cause will a man leave his father and mother
> and be united to his wife?   //

It's funny how often the disciples think Jesus is talking about one thing, when in reality He's talking about something completely different. One day they're in a boat heading across the lake when Jesus says, "Be careful. Be on your guard against the yeast of the Pharisees and Sadducees."[2] He's talking about their influence on the disciples, of course—but the disciples grow worried about bread.[3]

Note to self, they're thinking, *if anyone offers us bread, "just say no."*

But Jesus is speaking more as a poet than they realize.

The apostle Paul picked up God's love of metaphors when he wrote to the Ephesians, "For this cause a man will leave his father and mother and be united to his wife, and the two will become one flesh."[4] Paul had just been writing to the Ephesians about the relationship between husbands and wives, so it's natural for us to think "this cause" is about…well, *our* relationship. Our future together as a married couple. Isn't it? After all, everything about an engagement and a wedding is about the bride (and sorta the groom.) *Marriage*. Isn't that what Paul is talking about?

Yes…and no.

You see, "this cause" denotes a substitution relationship—using one thing to better understand another. We often pass right by the verse before, in which the apostle Paul wrote "no one ever hated his body, but he feeds and cares for it, *just as Christ does the church [italics: mine]*." "This cause" is not about us—not about our own marriage here on earth, though that provides perhaps the closest picture of that reality. It's about God and His relationship to His church. "This cause" is *God's* cause, the ultimate fulfillment of our covenant relationship with our Heavenly Father.

2   Matthew 16:6
3   Which is understandable. As devout Jews they were concerned with matters of ritual purity.
4   Ephesians 5:31, a verse that echoes Genesis 2:24.

Think of it like this. I (Byron) was watching a golf long-drive competition on TV, and it was amazing how much emphasis they placed on the club head speed produced by the swing: proper grip on the club; proper stance with your feet; timely and rapid shoulder rotation, coordinated with the arms training the wrists to snap and roll just right. They went on and on describing the perfect swing.

But then it hit me,

when it comes down to it,

the swing is all about

making proper contact with the ball.

Preparation for the end result.

Golf and life contain some great spiritual metaphors. But I use a metaphor because God is fond of using them. You get the feeling that way back, before the beginning of time, when God was creating the world, perhaps part of His purpose in creating marriage was to provide a poetic metaphor for our relationship with Him. In the same way that my golf swing isn't just about the swing—it's all about making contact with the ball—our earthly marriage is preparation for that eternal connection to our Creator forever and ever. That's why earthly marriage is *before* the consummation of that *forever* covenant with God. And just as my golf swing pales in comparison as a metaphor to learning how to be in covenant relationships,[5] so earthly marriage pales in comparison to that heavenly-forever relationship.

For when *that* day comes, it will be the perfect wedding feast[6] as Scripture calls it, made perfect by the sacrificial preparation of Christ.

....

5   My golf swing pales in comparison to a lot of things....
6   Matthew 22:2,3; John 2:1-10; John 3:29

Commitment. Covenant. What's the Difference?

// What's the difference between a commitment and a covenant? //

No doubt you're committed to your partner. You're probably growing more and more fluent in her "love languages." She's growing more fluent in yours. You seem to have all the ingredients that *soft-focus, slow-motion, running-through-the-fields-of-wildflowers* commercials are made of.

But how do you both respond when one of you is no longer getting what you want?

That's when the difference between a commitment and a covenant makes all the difference. A commitment is a contract of sorts that is man-made and can be renegotiated by the agreement of both parties. Remember that loan Carla and I got early in our married life when our car's air conditioner went out? The contract allowed the car dealer to get what he wanted, the bank to get what it wanted, and us to get what we wanted.[7] As long as we continued to pay our end of the deal, everyone was happy.[8]

A covenant, on the other hand, is not only usually legally binding; it is also spiritually binding. A contract is written on paper, whereas a covenant is written on human hearts, formed by the mingling of souls. A contract is often notarized by a public official as its witness, but for a covenant that witness is God Himself.

A marriage, then, is much, much more than simply two people receiving a license to live together. It is a covenant agreement instituted by God. Covenant literally means "a cutting, with reference to the dividing of animals into two parts, and the contracting parties passing between the two pieces of flesh in making an agreement,"[9] with the Hebrew word picture of flesh joining, of hearts meshing and being super(naturally)-glued together, which nothing but death can separate. Marriage then is an earthly picture of the divine relationship between God's

---

7   Until hindsight later proved that, because of our interest payments, the two of them had gotten the better end of the deal.
8   Especially the loan lender and car dealer. Okay, enough already....
9   *Easton's Bible Dictionary.* Public Domain. 18 March 2008 <http://eastonsbibledictionary.com/>.

bride—His church—and God Himself, who "remembers his covenant forever, the word he commanded, for a thousand generations."[10]

Commitment probably wouldn't be so difficult to commit to if we were less focused on ourselves and if our lives were more characterized by sacrificial love from the beginning. After all, that was God's original intent when He created us. That's what we've been working back toward, what God has been helping us toward through His sacrifice.

And *that* kind of God-modeled commitment—*sacrifice*—makes all the difference in helping us find the way back to what He intended our relationships to be.

10   1 Chronicles 16:15 & Psalm 105:8

015 how much baggage am I willing to carry?

....

For months I'd kept our honeymoon destination a surprise from Carla. All I would reveal was that maybe we were heading to "the mountains," maybe "the beach." I finally told her a few weeks before to pack her bikini for the sun. On our wedding night I revealed the destination.

Ixtapa, Mexico!

It was Carla's first trip out of the country and since she had no idea where she was headed, she wanted to make sure she had everything she needed. And because it's not every day that I get to go to Ixtapa, I packed everything I thought I'd need, including my golf clubs and probably two suitcases too many.[1] Between the two of us I think we could have opened a small sporting goods and clothing boutique with all we were taking with us. Finally the morning came that we were to leave… and everything that could go wrong did go wrong.

The restaurant burned breakfast.

We got caught behind a painfully slow truck on a two-lane highway.

While taking one of my infamous "short cuts," we lost even more time.

The airport shuttle passed us by because the signal beacon at our pick-up station was broken.

....
1   All I really needed was a Speedo…but Carla would not let me wear one.

Needless to say, by the time we finally got to the terminal, we were running late. *Very* late. With only minutes remaining until the airline closed the door for boarding, we sprinted for the elevator. I crammed my luggage on the elevator, then turned to grab Carla's stuff just in time…

…to   see
                    the   door
                    close.

I unloaded my suitcases on the upper floor and stood there for what seemed like an eternity waiting for Carla to appear. And when the elevator door finally opened, there she stood in tears.

It wasn't exactly the romantic beginning to our honeymoon we'd envisioned. We missed our flight and spent twelve hours in the airport, kicking off what turned out to be the honeymoon from hell.

But that is another story….

Bearing One Another's Burdens.

//   What does it mean to bear each other's burdens?   //

Byron and I learned a lesson that day. Now when we fly somewhere, we travel much lighter. In many ways, that story about lugging all our stuff around illustrates both the benefits and difficulties of bearing one another's burdens. When I was carrying all my baggage, my heart was pumping, blood was racing through my body, and my muscles began to burn. It's difficult to rush through life hauling such a heap of baggage, and I wasn't exactly enjoying myself. But after the elevator incident, when Byron came alongside me and picked up my stuff for a time, allowing me to shake out my arms, my baggage wasn't nearly as heavy when I picked it up again.

In other words, when we help each other bear our burdens, we find ourselves able to continue on in the struggles of life. The apostle Paul affirmed this when he wrote to the Galatians,

> Brothers, if someone is caught in a sin, you who are spiritual should restore him gently. But watch yourself, or you also may be tempted. Carry each other's burdens, and in this way you will fulfill the law of Christ. If anyone thinks he is something when he is nothing, he deceives himself. Each one should test his own actions. Then he can take pride in himself, without comparing himself to somebody else, for each one should carry his own load.[2]

All of us face difficulties in this world…and not just because of our own sin. We also wrestle with the sins committed against us as well as the mundane, everyday pressures of life, all of which combine to weigh us down. And when those around us mess up, the apostle Paul says that we are to "restore" them gently.

That word *restore* means to return something to the way it was, just as we would set a broken bone or mend a fishing net. Restoration is something we all need, because though we were all created in the image of God, that image has been marred by the effects of sin in the world. The wonderful reality of human relationships, however, is that God can use people to help free us from the oppressive weight that entangles us.

To help return us to what we were created to be.

To help set our broken bones to run again.

To help lift those burdens.

To *restore* us.

That's important, because in order to have a healthy marriage you must be able to lean on each other, to help carry your partner's weight from time to time and

---

2   Galatians 6:1-5

to allow that other person to carry your weight as well. In order to be a good "burden carrier," take the previous chapters seriously. Take time to consider your fears and desires pressing on you to be married. Take time to consider your own foundation and your expectations. In other words, you have to know yourself and what weighs *you* down. Our personal baggage (junk) has to come out in the open. I had to become vulnerable about what I had been carrying through life, and I had to get to know Byron and what weighs him down.

Both of us have to be aware of the ways God is helping us bear each other's burdens.

Take Time to Get to Know Them (and Their Baggage).

// How can I assess my partner's baggage? //

Assessing these things, of course, takes time, and you not only need to watch that other person's character over time; you need time to watch their character in person. If your relationship consists mainly of IM'ing each other three states away, it's difficult to really get to know that other person. Character is difficult to assess when you're not around watching both the *up*'s and *down*'s of their life.

We've known couples who have dated long distance. At times that may be necessary when one is serving overseas in the military, studying abroad, working jobs in different cities, etc. But long-distance dating is certainly not the best way to get to know someone. And if you're going to get married, we'd go so far as to say that it's crucial to be in the same place for a while, because time, being together, and face-to-face communication are essential to really getting to know the other person from the inside out. That's the only way that you're going to be able to answer the following questions:

Is he willing to sacrifice for you?

Is she interested only in what she gets out of the relationship?

Am I around him enough to know that there are no major addictions or past abusive situations he might be hiding?

Hiding Out.

// Are you or your partner hiding undealt-with pain? //

Twenty-seven years ago, Richard married his beautiful bride, Trent. "For years," she said, "he served as a deacon and elder in the same church in which we were married." Yet Richard had baggage (secrets and anger) from his early years that was unresolved. As a result, he was extremely controlling in his relationship with Trent and created a performance-driven environment in his home and at work, decorating his exterior life with status and possessions. Because Richard couldn't deal with the reality of his pain, he created illusions to avoid revealing his true self.

He put on a mask and began bluffing.

Hiding out.

Holding onto his mask at all costs. Costs that were high and growing higher.

He was ashamed to tell his wife of their financial troubles, and instead of seeking help, he borrowed significant amounts of money without telling her.

Ultimately, they went completely broke.

When he got to the end of his rope, he finally realized that the pain of being in the open is far less than the pain of hiding out.

You see, earlier in his life Richard experienced different types of abuse. When he came to Christ in the mid-1970's, he ascribed to the simplistic notion of "forgive and forget" (read, "forgive" and shove down), avoiding the deep, layer-by-layer work necessary for true forgiveness. "I wasn't fooling anyone except myself," Richard said.

"And for sure I was not fooling God!" He feared opening his past because he had lost confidence that anyone, including God, could help. "Whether the unresolved sin was by me or a sin against me," he told us, "the outcome was the same. It had an inevitable effect that equaled shame and/or guilt."

At the beginning of Richard and Trent's journey into healing, a Christian counselor taught them to keep that process in the light—in the open and always out in front—and to trust God to use each other to demonstrate His love. That deep transparency and care was important to his restoration, for as Richard pointed out a person cannot build a new house on the ruins of an old foundation.

into-me-see & "perfect love casts out fear..." | p.060 & 061

If you see character issues in your partner's life, don't look away or into the future to what "could be." Face those issues head-on. If you don't face them now, you'll face them later; eventually you have to work through them. *Can you live with what you see or do you expect him or her to change?* That's an important question to answer because, on average, a person will change only a small percentage after getting married.

Love may always hope, but if your love is dependant on your hope for your partner's change—on what *might be* rather than what *is*—what kind of a love is it that is based in fantasy rather than in reality?

What kind of a *relationship* is that?

Are *You* Healthy Enough to Carry Your Own Burden?

//   Why is it important to carry my own baggage?   //

How much baggage am I willing to carry? The answer, if I were to be honest with myself—if any of us are to be really honest with our self—is probably *as little as possible.* Given the selfish choice, I'd rather carry as little of my baggage and as little of Carla's baggage as possible. Traveling ultra light or, better yet, having someone else carry my stuff sounds pretty good.

But that's where trouble creeps in.

You see, if I expect Carla to carry all my baggage at the airport as well as hers, it's not only Carla's *muscles* that will soon be burning. When it comes to bearing each other's burdens, our unrealistic expectations can get the best of us. I can't pack my golf clubs and snorkel gear and cram my suitcases full for Mexico and expect Carla to carry them all in addition to her stuff, just as I can't expect her to carry me in my life where I'm struggling. We all carry baggage through life, but when I expect Carla or anyone else to bear *my* burdens—to be my personal porter carrying what weighs me down—I'm shirking a responsibility that Scripture says is mine.

"*Carry each other's burdens,*" the apostle Paul wrote. Then, only a few verses later, "*each one should carry his own load.*" Those two words he used, *burdens* and *load*, aren't just synonyms for the same term. In the Greek, they are in fact different words. While the first word we translate "burdens" implies something closer to a weight naturally requiring assistance, that second word, *load*, refers more to "one's proper burden."[3] And *that* load is my responsibility, not Carla's.

Imagine how it would go over if a climbing team were high on Mt. Everest in what is known as the "death zone," and one of the team members suddenly radios down, "I'm not going to carry my pack anymore."

"What's wrong?" the team doctor radios back from Base Camp. "Are you suffering from high-altitude sickness?"

"No."

"Pulmonary edema? Do you find your lungs filling up with fluid?"

"No."

"Then what?"

"Well, I was just thinking that I don't really want to carry my stuff anymore."

---

3   Fung, Ronald Y. K. *The Epistle to the Galatians.* (Grand Rapids: William B. Eerdmans, 1988): 291.

Now understand, that team is ready to rescue anyone on the mountain facing the overwhelming *burdens* of high-altitude climbing and will risk their own lives to help *restore* them if they need that. But simply not carrying your own *load* because you don't want to is not going to go over very well.

If you want to marry, you need to be the kind of person willing to do the hard work of, as the apostle put it, "carrying his own load." You need to not only identify what your own baggage is—you need to pick up your own duties and carry them out. So give yourself a quick "gut check" of your character and ask yourself, *am I willing to carry my own load, my own pack? Is my partner willing to carry his or her own load?*

Can't See Around Your Own Baggage?

//   Is my own baggage affecting my ability to see
my relationship objectively?   //

The questions above are important ones to ask both of yourself and your partner, because if our own baggage is weighing us down, we might not be able to help carry our partner's baggage, let alone see around the pile we're carrying. If you tend to rescue people, for example—if you are someone who habitually seeks out troubled people to offer help—you may find yourself in a relationship with a person in need of rescuing. We've seen couples in which one or the other person was drawn to help their partner who struggled with drug abuse or money mismanagement. It's easy for the rescuer to defend the other person by hiding behind a Scriptural mandate. But just because you're ministering to someone—having faith in them, hoping for change, and believing in their journey—certainly doesn't mean you should marry them.

Marriage always requires ministry to your mate, but just because you're ministering to a person in need, don't be fooled into thinking this person needs you *till death do you part.*

Others are blinded not by their over-enthusiasm to rescue people, but by one of the most dangerous of sins: *pride*. "*If anyone thinks he is something when he is nothing,*" the apostle Paul wrote in Galatians 6:3, "*he deceives himself.*" And pride, thinking you are something when you're not, is heavy baggage. Because if your life is characterized by pride and judgment rather than understanding and grace, you won't be able to sympathize, comfort, and come alongside your partner. People dealing with pride in this way sometimes effectively cross Galatians 6:2 out of their Bibles with a black Sharpie pen, not "carrying each other's burdens," which they see as a sign of weakness.

Ironically, they are the ones weak inside.

For years, Richard could not see around his own baggage. He thought it was up to him to hold life together with bailing wire and duct tape, to cope with the symptoms as best he could instead of going to the root of his problems. Consequently, he didn't have time or energy for anyone. It wasn't until he got to the end of his rope that he sought help; only then was he able to begin helping others.

Often we can't identify our weaknesses alone, of course; we need others' help to shine light deep into who we are. When you're carrying your own stuff, it's sometimes difficult to see around that tower of baggage. But asking others for help in this area is a perfect example of what God intended when He pointed out our need in the first place to bear each other's burdens.

Bearing Burdens Takes Sacrifice.

//   Am I willing to sacrifice my expectations for my partner?   //

If you haven't already got the memo running throughout this entire chapter, bearing your own burden and helping bear the burden of your partner takes sacrifice.

Lots of sacrifice.

commitment's easy. (it's sacrifice that's difficult.) & roadblock ahead: what's stopping you from sacrifice? | p.155 & 156

I have tried over the years of our marriage to "make" Byron relate to God as I do. Over time, that expectation became extra weight for him to carry around. But once I gave up that desire for him to be like me, it released that weight in his life and mine. Likewise, Byron was obsessed with football in his younger years. Football was his god, what made him "significant." Thankfully, he has dealt with who he is and what gives him significance. It is certainly not his football performance or living vicariously through others on the field. Today he's totally changed in that area from when we were dating, and that sacrifice of his has released what could have been a burden in our life together.

Those are small things when considered alongside other, much larger sacrifices that many couples make. For some couples, sacrifice will involve letting go of family to form a new family. For others it might be giving up hobbies that interfere with family life, dealing with abuse or neglect, or a multitude of other issues. Everyone's story will be different; every couple will have different things to sacrifice in order for the two to become one.

This can all sound pretty heavy, but Jesus once told a crowd of people that his burden is easy and yoke is light.[4] Which, if we're following Him in all aspects of our lives, including the way we relate to one another, is what our relationship should be as well.

Hard, demanding *work*, but an easy *burden*.

A light yoke.

4   Matthew 11:28-30

016 is it time to consider moving from commitment to covenant?

....

In previous generations, if a couple was engaged and the man backed out of the deal, the woman could bring legal action against him for lost time and damage to her future marriage prospects. If it looked like the guy was sitting back, twiddling his thumbs—afraid of commitment or moving too slowly—the young woman's parents would often sit the man down to ask what "his intentions" were.[1] Wow... that's intense?

Wow. And you thought *your* steps to deeper commitment were intense.

Times have changed, and though engagement stories no longer sound as if they're straight out of a Jane Austen novel, one thing remains constant: there comes a moment in which you've considered all you know about yourself, all you know about your partner, all you know about God and His ways and what He's calling you both to—and you have to make a choice. Do you move forward into marriage or do you call it off? Do you "know that you know" enough to step forward?

Not more hypothetical questions here; we're asking you that question. Do *you* "know that you know" enough to step forward in this relationship?

Is it time for you to consider moving from commitment to covenant?

---

1   Landis, Judson T. and Mary G. *Building a Successful Marriage.* (Englewood Cliffs: Prentice-Hall, Inc., 1948): 223.

No Longer *"Me"*…But *"Us."*

//   How do my loyalties shift as we move toward engagement
and into marriage?   //

Whenever Byron and I begin a new pre-engagement class, that first evening we like to remind couples about the new unit that is formed when two become one.

Marriage is no longer about me, we tell them.

It's about us.

It's no longer me, but we.

Though you still are separate individuals, of course, when you marry you begin to share an identity in a unique way—spiritually, legally, emotionally, sexually—in all facets of who you are as human beings.

Life changes when you move from commitment to covenant. You give up some independence, but gain a wonderful companion to travel through life with. You give up some of your individual freedom to do what you want when you want, but you gain freedom through the acceptance and love of your spouse. The Old Testament book of Genesis describes this process of transferring loyalties as "leaving and cleaving."

Byron officiated a wedding in which the father of the bride was very close to his tom-boy daughter—even a bit over-protective of her. "I tried to run the guy off in high school," he admitted to us, "but I started warming up to him when I found that he was also as dedicated to his sports as she is to hers." The couple dated through college before deciding to marry, and for both sets of parents, it was clearly difficult to allow the shift of loyalties as their children's relationship moved toward marriage.[2]

....

2   Author and educator Dr. Stephen Glenn says the weaning process is difficult for both the wean-ee and the wean-or. In other words, during the process of engagement it is just as difficult for the parents to let go as it is for their children—*you*—to jump out of the nest into full responsibility.

If you've ever had a close friend get married, you probably know what we're talking about. Your friend may have grown preoccupied, more distant. You may have even felt like you were losing your friend.

In a way, you were. You may lose time together, primary allegiance, and shared intimacy as your friend "leaves and cleaves" to her spouse. A radical shift occurs when you step into marriage, transferring allegiances and affections. The process may feel difficult at times, but leaving and cleaving is normal and a natural part of the covenant process.

That's why parents often go through a tough adjustment during the engagement period. But notice, however, where they sit at a wedding. The sets of parents are strategically positioned on the front row—the best courtside seats in the house—not only because they've given so much love, time, and effort into raising those two people, but also because their role going forward becomes that of being the couple's biggest cheerleaders. The parents cannot play the game of life for the newlyweds; they no longer call the shots. And in order to be successful as a team themselves, every married couple must "leave father and mother and cleave" to one another through their covenantal commitment.

To do that, it's important to look to your firm foundation, the Creator of the marriage covenant—God. Because marriage is His idea.

Covenant is His idea.

Leaving and cleaving is His idea.

So chances are He has something to say on the subject to help you through the transition.

Entrusted With a Great Responsibility.

//   How can we know God's will for our relationship?   //

"I know God won't give me anything I can't handle," Mother Teresa once said of her demanding work with Calcutta's Missionaries of Charity. "I just wish He didn't trust me so much!"[3]

God has entrusted you, too, with a great responsibility: the decision whom to marry. You, too, may wish that He didn't trust you so much, but that very act shows God's great confidence in you. Seriously dating Christian couples will most likely at some point ask the question, *how do I know what God's will is?* It's a great question that by itself could fill books. Many books, in fact, have been written about that very question.[4] We could summarize the points you may have heard before: that God often confirms His will through His word (Scripture); otherwise, mature believers; tradition passed down through the community of faith; circumstances; and inner peace about a particular decision.

But a lot comes down to this.

Any good parent will entrust his or her child with greater and greater responsibility to help that child mature into an adult. Sure, it's a lot easier to have your parents make decisions for you (and when you're young, it's often easier for them to do that simply to save time and hassle). But instead they teach you how to pick up after yourself and wash your own laundry[5] and make your own decisions so that you'll mature.

God does the same for us through our life's daily challenges, bringing us from immaturity to maturity through the decisions, tensions, and pressures we face. And the decision of whether or not you should marry figures prominently in your spiritual formation. Understanding God's will for your relationship is really less about identifying the one, "right" person for you (as if such a thing existed), and

---

3   http://www.anecdotage.com/index.php?aid=13617
4   In fact, we'd recommend you read one of them. Kyle Lake's book *Understanding God's Will: How to Hack the Equation Without Formulas.* (Orlando: Relevant Books, 2005).
5   Though most single guys I know are still growing in these first two areas....

instead learning to make wise decisions within God's principles. God wants us to grow and part of that growth involves learning to make decisions in a healthy way.

Because He loves us. Because He believes in us.

Like Mother Teresa, you may wish God didn't trust you so much. That He would just give you a slip of paper with some name on it with whom to marry. But that would be too easy. And God has bigger plans for you. He believes that you're capable of making this decision. He knows that if you seek diligently, you too can move into the covenant knowing that you know. And He wants to give you the chance to grow through this process.

It is a big responsibility, but with His help, *you* can rise to the occasion.

He already knows that.

What's the Rush?

//   If I have doubts about my relationship, why not slow down?
What's the rush?   //

Imagine a couple—let's call them Stacy and Jeff. They've been dating for nearly two years and have talked about taking a pre-engagement class at their church. Recently, however, Jeff met a woman that...

rocked

his

world.

Everything that Jeff found Stacy lacking—outgoingness toward people and a sense of purpose—Julia had in abundance. And so Jeff found himself wondering, *is Stacy really God's best for me? Should I stay committed to this relationship I've been in for nearly two years? Or is Julia a better match? Could my attraction for Julia simply be infatuation?*

"beauty" > chaos > real beauty | p.011

In other words, *is it okay to test my level of commitment with different people before marriage?*

If you're in this situation, and you're considering that, yes, testing the relationship by stepping back from your relationship and spending time with another person might be a good idea, then you know what? Perhaps you should. Those questions have a way of being a "gut check" for you, shining that searching light into the dark, innermost places of your life. They force you to inner conversations you need to have with yourself and with God. Of course, whatever you choose will have ramifications. You can't tell your girlfriend that you'd like to step back for a while so that you can date other women without that having consequences.

If you're not completely confident about your relationship, what's the rush? Slow down and think your relationship through, because your decision whom you're going to marry is incredibly important.

If you're considering a lifelong future together and you're not certain you should get married, why move forward now?

We've met so many couples in a rush—and usually the ones in the greatest rush are those carrying the heaviest burdens. They want to fix their situation and *quickly*! (Get me out of this house with my parents! Show me some financial stability! Give me an outlet for my sex drive!)

why do I want to be married so badly? | p.045

They use verses out of context to justify their actions, but if they were to stop and evaluate their own hearts, they'd find that it would be better to slow down than speed up. My favorite line, as we talked about earlier, is when a guy tosses out the ol'"it is better to marry than burn with lust" line instead of slowing down and learning self-control.

You'll have to sift through your fears, preferably with a friend or pastor who can give you a wise, mature, objective perspective. You may be unsure about your partner's behavior, or unsure if they're hiding something from you. *Do you feel trapped in your relationship? Are your fears grounded in reality? Or do they just feel real?*

When I (Carla) was thinking through whether to move from commitment to covenant, I asked myself, can I see myself married to anyone else? And I really couldn't. If there were anyone else around other than Byron, I was oblivious. Did that mean that I wouldn't meet anyone smarter or better looking or more confident than Byron after I married?[6] Did that mean I wouldn't meet other wonderful men after our wedding day?

No.

What it did mean, however, is that I wouldn't meet anyone more *Byron* than Byron. No one else had the exact combination of traits that he did. No one would ever be more *Byron* than Byron. And I wanted to be married to Byron—all of Byron—for I felt more myself together with him than apart.

So if, as you look around, you can see yourself married to someone else—or if you have serious hesitations—take time. Slow down. When it's your entire married life ahead of you that you're talking about, what's the rush?

Laying it All Out Before God.

The Old Testament hero of faith, Abraham, was facing his greatest challenge. Years before, he'd heard and responded to God's call to leave his hometown of Ur and set out for the land promised to him by God. And he'd followed through. He'd held onto God's promise that he'd bear a child who would be the father of many nations. He'd also messed up along the way, doing things his way instead of God's way. But now God was doing the unthinkable—asking him to give up his promised son, the one whose lineage would create a great nation.

6　Byron's comment: *"Like she could even find a better looking, smarter guy than me. But I guess I just proved the 'lacking confidence' part…."*

It was a mind-boggling request, and as Abraham was walking up the mountain with his son Isaac, he surely considered the sacrifice in agonizing detail. Because the sacrifice that they were going to offer—that had been requested by God—was the life of his own son. And not just any son. "Your son," God says, "your only son, Isaac, whom you love." Abraham's mind must have been going back over and over the request, like a scratched CD that keeps playing the same seven-second sound bite.

That kid meant the world to Abraham. He knew the cost and knew he was at a point of no return with Isaac. He had deeply considered his conversations with God and was so moved by God that he was willing to pay whatever the cost.

The closest I can come to relating to what Abraham went through was when our only son, Bo, was fighting cancer. As a two-and-a-half-year-old, the little guy had been through radiation and chemo treatment, but his tumor hadn't melted away as we all hoped it would. So immediately after Christmas, he went in for surgery. The situation didn't look good, and the doctor was preparing us for the worst. He was saying things such as "if he makes it" and "if he survives," phrases that take root in a parent's mind and don't stop growing. The medical staff didn't know what they'd find when they opened him up; even if they were able to remove the tumor successfully, being under anesthetic for nine hours could kill the little guy.

When it was finally time to begin his surgery, the nurse let me carry him in until we reached a pair of double doors. "This is as far as I can let you go," she said, and there Carla and I prayed for Bo.

The nurse had to literally pry him out of my arms.

As I let him go, I wondered whether it would be the last time I ever held my son alive. We watched as the nurse took him down the hallway, which stretched on forever. Then she turned a corner and they were gone.

Carla and I stood there, our faces pressed against the glass, as we embraced and cried. After awhile, we went to the hospital chapel, where we prayed together. As we did, the thought flashed into my mind that what we were going through must be just a glimpse of what Abraham went through as he walked up the mountain with his son Isaac. Like Abraham, we were putting our son into God's hands.

Abraham was willing to lay it all at that altar. He believed trusting God was worth the risk. Which was a bit of what we felt in that hospital chapel as we prayed. When we left, we had an inexplicable peace that this nine-hour surgery was going to be okay...*even if Bo didn't make it.*

In taking the step of faith that Abraham did, he was moving more deeply into that covenant relationship, knowing that from all he'd seen of God, he could trust Him. And so he was going all in, not half-hearted.

Saying *yes* to God.

Taking that step of faith.

Finally doing things God's way, not his own.

Knowing that even during times of doubt,

God knows best.

/////////////

O MOST HIGH, GLORIOUS GOD, enlighten the darkness of my heart and give me
> a right faith,
>> a certain hope
>>> and a perfect love,
>>>> understanding and knowledge,

O LORD,
> That I may carry out your holy and true command.

Amen.

-St. Francis of Assisi

Now that you are at the end of this section, take time to reflect on what sacrifice really looks like for a couple considering marriage. Perhaps watch a sporting event together or at least think through the dynamics that take place. Afterward discuss the various levels of commitment and sacrifice made by the coaches…and the players…and the trainers/managers…and the support staff. Why are athletics such a visual of sacrifice, teamwork, and commitment? What kind of sacrifice is demanded of a good team player? Are you prepared to make that type of commitment for your future marriage?

consider the __sacrifice

section_06
consider the future

017 are our parents for or against it?
does it really matter?

....

When you marry, people say, you don't just marry your partner, you marry two families. Which is true. You're not just entering into a relationship with your spouse; you're entering into ongoing, life-long relationships with your in-laws as well.

But it's also true that as you cleave to your mate, you *leave* your parents. When you marry you create a new family of your own. A separate spiritual unit. It's the *two* that become one.

Not the *six*.

Not the *eleven*.

This can create a tricky middle ground to navigate if one or both of your parents disagrees with the two of you about whether you should get married.

How then do you make sense of any disagreements with those close to you?

Look to Those Looking Out for You.

// How important is it that our friends and family are excited
about the match?   //

Awhile back there was a couple in our pre-engagement class who had met at college and dated thousands of miles away from their close friends and family. As the couple began to think about tying the knot, family and friends back home began to worry about their decision. The potential bride's parents as well as her close girlfriend back home all thought she was moving too fast. But Shermane kept insisting, "No, you have to trust me. This is the guy."

Because of the great distance between them, trust was all Shermane's family and friends could do. There was no chance for any of them to really get to know Eric. *We trust* you, the family found themselves replying, *but we simply don't know this guy, and that makes us a bit nervous.*

With so many people who love them, that couple would have been foolish to ignore everyone's concern, because their relationship with each other wasn't the only thing in focus. There were also relationships with parents, brothers, sisters, other family members, and friends who cared deeply about them. When a relationship feels like it's a match made in heaven, however, it's easy to mistakenly forsake other relationships (at least temporarily) for "*The Relationship*" in front of you. But remember, as we've seen over the past chapters, a match that feels like it's made in heaven isn't necessarily the case. There are all sorts of reasons why we're drawn into particular relationships, so it's a bit naïve (and, if you're honest with yourself, arrogant) to think that those who love you—who have seen your life over the years and who probably care about your well being more than any others—don't have anything valid to say to you when it comes to this incredibly life-changing relationship in your life.

Instead, take time to look to those looking out for you. Because if he really is such a great guy, all it would take is a little time for them to get to know him. Do whatever you can to allow family and friends to get to know that person you're with. Sure, this is a season in your life in which your loyalties are shifting, but don't cut yourself off from those who have already been loyal to you.

Ask yourself, *why would I* not *want the support of my friends and family regarding this relationship?* Keep the big, long-term picture in mind. When we sent out an informal survey to those who receive our ministry newsletter, asking them how many of them had the support of friends and family (among other questions), 97% of those who responded said they did have that support.

For Eric and Shermane's parents and friends to get to know Eric, it would have cost money and they would have had to fly across the country. But that's money well spent. Spend both the needed *time* and *money* to encourage that interaction with friends and family before you spend your *life* together. Because, believe us, the price of a couple of round-trip plane tickets plus expenses—as expensive as that might feel to you right now—is a lot less expensive than the emotional cost of an entire life together that…well, really wasn't the best idea.

For some of you, however, that may still raise the question, *but what if they still don't like the person?*

Does Honoring Your Parents Mean Obeying Them?

//   Do honoring parents and obeying them go hand in hand?   //

I (Byron) recently officiated a wedding one weekend where the relationship between the groom and his father was strained. As a result, Tim hadn't seen his father in quite some time, yet as we neared the beginning of the wedding, his estranged father unexpectedly walked into the church.

Which could have been a disaster—or at the very least an awkward, tense situation.

But Tim did a wonderful thing. He sat down with his father in a back room and talked with him for probably 15-20 minutes. At the end of that time, they hugged. Throughout the entire service his father sat quietly without causing any trouble.

In spite of his past actions—the things he had done to cause alienation within the family—that father simply wanted to see his son get married. Tim very graciously honored his father, and that kind of second-chance love didn't give Satan a foothold into destroying the family even more.

Of course, it doesn't always work out so neatly. But whether you have a close relationship with your parents now or not, *work toward that relationship by loving and honoring your parents.* If you haven't talked about your disagreements openly, do it. Sit down and have an honest conversation. Or write them a letter to open dialogue.

When parents are actively involved in their children's lives, of course, they'll probably have relational capital to offer their opinions. But many parents today unfortunately aren't very involved in their children's lives, and as we grow into adults, we increasingly come to see that everyone, including our parents, has baggage. Unfortunately, parents' baggage—controlling behavior, unreasonable expectations for their children, and immature behavior—can sometimes surface during the engagement period. Put bluntly, some parents can even be less mature than their own children.

So if you've considered what they have to say, you've weighed their judgments by getting outside perspectives—and they still refuse to "give you their blessing" on your relationship—can you honor your parents without obeying them?

In Paul's letter to the Ephesians he wrote, "Children, obey your parents in the Lord, for this is right."[1] That word "obey" is said "of one who on a knock at the door comes to listen who it is."[2] Paul continues by quoting the Old Testament book of Exodus, "'Honor your father and mother'—which is the first commandment with a promise—'that it may go well with you and that you may enjoy long life on this earth.'"[3]

1   Ephesians 6:1
2   Earle, Ralph. *Word Meanings in the New Testament.* (Grand Rapids: Baker Book House, 1991): 325. Citing Thayer, J. H. *A Greek-English Lexicon of the New Testament.* (New York: American Book Co., 1886)
3   Ephesians 6:2-3, quoting Exodus 20:12

Going against the wishes of your parents and marrying someone they're not thrilled about is a difficult decision, of course, and one to weigh with your friends, pastor, and other family members. Making that kind of decision requires wisdom; it's not a decision you should make on your own. *Are you truly listening to your parents, going to the door of your inner thoughts to listen to what they have to say? Are you honoring them by doing that?*

If you've taken those steps with your partner before others and before God, in the end, you can value your parents deeply, listen to them well, and truly love them—but that doesn't mean you are bound to obey them if you are convinced that their opinions are off base.

Avoid Triangulation.

> //   What if my parents still don't like my partner after all we've tried?
> How do we handle the differences?   //

Search hard enough with anyone and you'll probably find *something* you disagree with. But it's difficult when those disagreements are with the ones you most want on your side: your parents. It's even more difficult when it's about your choice of a future spouse.

Sometimes cultural expectations differ between you and your parents. They may not think you're old enough to get married. They may have their own prejudices regarding your boyfriend's or girlfriend's socio-economic level or education—or they may have outright racial prejudices. Whatever the issue—no matter how much you disagree with their views, their prejudice, perhaps even their hatred—strive to honor them in how you speak to them or about them.

We have seen how difficult this can be among the couples we know. When conflict does occur between you as a couple and one or both of your sets of parents, be aware of creating barriers between family members by triangulation, when three parties are involved in a *he said/she said* disagreement. Usually one says something about the other to a third party instead of going directly to the other person.

Again, sit down and talk respectfully face to face with them about what you sense coming between you. Your parents may have valid concerns about your age or your ability to earn enough to support the two of you. Listen, especially if you are hearing the same message from others.

It's difficult; there's no doubt about that. But by showing them respect—regardless of how they respond—you're creating a new legacy of your own.

Create a New Legacy.

//   What if there's simply no way around the fact that my parents aren't
supporting what others are saying is a great match?
How do we handle it going forward into marriage?   //

When a father rejects the guy his daughter is engaged to because he doesn't meet his expectations, he probably isn't thinking much about how that might impact his relationship with both of them. When a mother leaves a father for another man and generally makes a mess of family life, she probably isn't thinking about the full consequences of her actions down the road with her children. And when a father abuses alcohol and loses control of himself, he probably isn't thinking down the road to being unwelcome at his son's wedding.

It would be easy to respond vindictively to any pain you've been dealt, making them hurt where they'll feel it:

Silence.

Withdrawal.

Lashing back with hurtful words.

Striving to resist "returning the favor" in the face of a trying relationship with your parents or future in-laws is a test of your love. We aren't saying it's easy to love in such situations. But then, God never said love would be easy.

When faced with difficult circumstances, will you still show Christ-like love to those around you?

You'll need to set healthy, appropriate boundaries, of course, so that you aren't hurt again. And as you strive to honor your parents—no matter how well you get along with them or how enthusiastic they are about your relationship—remember that you can't change them or their response. The only thing you can change is your response.

So instead, whatever the legacy you've received from your parents, work toward creating a new legacy in your own life, whether you decide to remain single or you decide to marry. *What do you wish your relationship with your parents could have been? What will you do to make your relationships look like that?*

As you strive to honor your parents, remember Paul's admonition earlier in Ephesians to "be imitators of Christ" and "live a life of love, just as Christ loved us." Because if you're able to develop this kind of mature love for your in-laws who may be making your life miserable…

…then just think of the kind of love you'll be able to show your future spouse.

018 do I have my "stuff" together?

....

One year, during a family vacation in Colorado, we all decided to pile in the van and drive up Pike's Peak for the views. We set off from Colorado Springs and as we saw it in the distance and I looked at the road signs telling us how many miles we had to the top, I thought, *that's not far away*. It would be an easy 10-15 minute drive to the summit.

Well, perhaps the high mountain air had something to do with either the van's gas consumption or my judgment, because by the time we reached the base of Pike's Peak, the gas gauge was on empty. I mentioned it to Carla, and then I reassured her and the kids, "Aw, don't worry about it. We can drive *way* past 'E.'"

I had proven on many occasions my faith in the auto makers, who always build in plenty of cushion for such situations. No doubt they discussed scenarios such as ours during research and development meetings. Plus, we couldn't be that far away from the summit. My friend Jim had run up Pike's Peak from the base in some kind of race—and he wasn't in the best shape—so it couldn't be far. If Jim could run up the mountain, sucking air, I told Carla and the kids, then surely our van could make it on fumes if it had to.

So we continued on.

As the mountain road continued to climb and the needle on the gas gauge continued to fall, I began to prop up my decision by jokingly telling the kids things such as "I could *push* this car up the mountain if I had to. No worries!" But inside I was beginning to doubt. We were about halfway up Pike's Peak and somehow the peak was drifting away…and it still didn't look like we were anywhere near making it. I began wondering, *Should I turn around?* Now Carla was worried. Worse still, she knew my track record: I'd run out of gas on more than one occasion with the family *in the vehicle.*

Yeah, *that's* how much faith I had in the auto maker's built-in cushion on the gas gauge.

Since we were about halfway up, I started wondering whether we should turn around and begin coasting down. *But then what if we were* over *halfway up? And what if there were a gas station at the top?* I began offering logical explanations to Carla and the kids about why we were continuing up. And when you begin rationalizing why the summit of Pike's Peak would make a great location for a gas station, you should realize that you're in trouble.

We hadn't fully counted the cost to see whether we could make it to the top. We didn't really have our stuff together to make the journey.[1]

Do You Have Your House in Order?

// Are we in a place to handle the practical demands of getting married? //

If you were a young Jewish man in ancient times, you had to earn your bride's rights. Although both fathers determined the arrangement, it was not uncommon for a young man to be required to work for years to pay a dowry for his new bride. This was not considered a payment or a purchase price for a wife, but compensation to the father for the loss of her help as a daughter. In addition, before a young man could bring home a wife, he first had to prepare to care for and protect her. This involved proving himself worthy of being a faithful man, building a proper house, and establishing the land to provide food. One could not hurry this process, and until construction was complete no marriage was going to take place. After the house and land were ready, the young man was finally ready to receive his bride.

....
1   Amazingly, we reached the summit (yes, we did reach it), but we had such a difficult time relaxing because we were all buzzing from the triple-shot adrenaline macchiato.

So, is your house and land ready?

I'm not talking about buying your dream house and taking up farming—or even renting an apartment. I'm talking about being deeply rooted and grounded as a person.

How do you know if you are ready or not?

Ask yourself these questions:
- *Am I ready and willing to do what it takes to enter a covenant relationship? With God? With a future mate?*
- *Have I adequately prepared myself?*
- *Am I whole and complete in Christ as a person?*

- *Am I stable enough spiritually? Emotionally? Mentally? Financially?*

you complete me—what does? | p.087

Rabbit Stew is a Whole Lot Less Expensive.

//   Have I considered the financial cost of getting married?   //

Awhile back I (Byron) read about "Four Common Financial Mistakes Young Couples Make":[2]

- Buying and selling cars
- Buying and selling houses
- Credit mismanagement due to a consumptive lifestyle
- Failing to calculate the cost of pets

Cars, houses, credit—it's easy to see how we can get into trouble with all those. But not accounting for pets?! On the surface, that may seem to be an odd one. But it's one Carla and I know from experience.

---

2   Burkett, Larry. *Complete Financial Guide for Young Couples: A Lifetime Approach to Spending, Saving and Investing.* (Colorado Springs: Chariot Victor Publishing, 1993).

When our kids were young, a family we knew gave us a rabbit as a pet. The kids loved it…but maybe a little too much. Because one day I looked out the back window and saw our four-year-old son, Bo, with the rabbit in his hands, pushing it down the slide. Which wasn't so unusual. Brittney, who was only about two years old at the time, was there at the bottom of the slide to "greet it," as she put it. Which also wasn't so unusual. But as I watched, Bo grabbed the rabbit and took it around to the top of the slide again and pushed it down. This time, when the rabbit got near the bottom of the slide, Brittney, overly enthusiastic about "greeting" the poor thing, suddenly flung the bottom of the slide up so that the rabbit went flying into the air like a movie stunt man, legs pumping for solid ground.

It limped (well, actually drug its hind legs) away from its *not-so-movie-stunt-man* landing, and so I went outside to check out the situation.

A broken leg.

At the time we were bringing in that big, six-figure youth minister's salary (with two of those figures to the right of the decimal point), so I feared vet-bill sticker shock. I told Carla I could "set" the leg by using popsicle sticks to splint it. She disagreed and called a veterinarian friend we knew. Before she could speak, I grabbed the phone.

"Hypothetically," I asked, "how much would it cost to splint a rabbit's leg?"

Her answer was exactly what I feared—about a hundred times more than what a rabbit is worth. So I asked if there were anything else we might be able to do, other than have it for dinner. Well, she said, you could create a soft cast for it with athletic tape. A roll of athletic tape was much closer to our price range, but at the time we didn't even have that, so I made a cast out of masking tape and left it on for a few weeks. It worked like a charm and the rabbit lived a long and healthy life.

If "not accounting for pets" figures into the financial pitfalls of newlyweds (how many of you calculated that one in?), just imagine all the other unseen financial pressures that might be out there. So if either you or your partner are irresponsible with money—or simply don't plan a budget—that should be a red flag to you both.

Do you know where your money's going?

We've seen many couples where one's a saver and the other's a spender—and that doesn't mean the saver's necessarily the one with the healthy patterns. He may save (read, *hoard*) because he trusts more in himself than God, and the spender, in fact, may be a very generous giver.[3] Author, speaker, and sociology professor at Eastern College, Tony Campolo, is fond of saying, "We buy things we don't need with money we don't have to impress people we don't know." I asked him about that quote over lunch when he spoke at Baylor, and he said he has added something to it: "…and people don't give a damn." Today, three out of four students borrow money for school, and the average B.A. student graduates with debt ranging from over $10,000 for public schools to over $24,000 for private schools.[4] Credit is little comfort; even a $10 pizza charged to your credit card will take approximately sixty months (five years) to pay off if you pay only the minimum payment each month.

It's no wonder then that roughly two-thirds of Christ's parables deal with financial matters, because he knew our tendency to turn $10 pizzas into budget nightmares. Scripture says that "where our treasure is, there our heart will be also," and the converse could probably also be said—that where our heart is, there are treasure is (or is spent) also. The inability to manage your money isn't just an economic issue; it's also a spiritual issue, reflecting your heart. So ask yourself these questions:

- Do I manage my money or does my money manage me?
- Have I learned delayed gratification? Do I have the discipline to wait?

Your attitude toward money provides a good "gut check" regarding your relationship with God, a window into where you're putting your trust. *Is it really "in God we trust," or are you placing your trust in the money it's printed on? Are you looking to money to*

---

3   Financial resources: www.crown.org, Dave Ramsey's book *Financial Peace*. (New York: Viking, 1997,) and www.daveramsey.com.

4   http://www.usatoday.com/money/perfi/general/2006-02-22-student-loans-usat_x.htm Posted 2/22/2006, Block, Sandra. "Students suffocate under tens of thousands in loans." *USA Today* online, citing College Board's 2005 Trends in Student Aid.

satisfy, or are you satisfied in Christ? Debt makes assumptions about the future and denies God the opportunity to work; if you're completely bound and gagged by debt, that restricts God's ability to use you, to send you where He wants, and to call on you to do His work.

But when you trust God, following His principles for your finances, that opens all kinds of possibilities for Him to work through.

Do You Have Your Stuff Together?

> //   After having considered all I can about our relationship,
> do I "have my stuff together"?
> Do any of us ever have our stuff all together?   //

His neighbors were pretty sure he didn't "have his stuff together." In fact, the neighbors probably thought Noah was missing quite a bit of stuff: *His mind, for one. Reason. Sanity.* I mean, seriously, who builds a giant boat in the middle of the desert?

God freak, they probably thought as they watched him.

But to God, the One who mattered, Noah was anything but a freak. On the contrary. In the book of Genesis we see that *"Noah found favor in the eyes of the LORD.... Noah was a righteous man, blameless among the people of his time, and he walked with God."⁵* Righteous. Blameless. Walking with God.

Noah, of course, didn't have much of a community of faith around him. Not a lot of people to run the big boat idea by; his family was really his only community of faith. Which is a pretty big difference between Noah and you. There are probably many around you who find favor in the eyes of the Lord. And so while God rarely speaks to us audibly as He did to Noah, He often speaks through those around us who are righteous.

---

5   Genesis 6:8-9

While his neighbors thought he'd "lost it," Noah had really found it.

Found his foundation.

Sacrificed in terms of his social standing.

Considered the future before him.

Do you have your stuff together? If by "having your stuff together" we mean being some model of perfection, then the answer is *no*. Of course you don't! None of us ever have all our stuff together this side of the full coming of God's Kingdom. Even our heroes of faith that we've described throughout this book didn't have their stuff together at various points in their lives, and often struggled deeply:

- *Abraham had a son by his wife's maidservant in an attempt to kick-start God's promise.*
- *Enoch went along with the deplorable values of his day before his 180-degree turn.*
- *Rahab was a prostitute among a pagan people before she ran into the arms of God.*
- *Moses killed a man while serving in the royal leadership of Egypt before responding to God's voice.*
- *The Israelites showed no shortage in doubting God as they headed to the Promised Land.*
- *And even after Noah had followed God and the ark had landed on dry land, he ended up in a perverse "Saints Gone Wild" scene, sprawled out in his tent, butt naked and passed out from binging on wine.*

Why in the world did these stories make it into our Bible? Perhaps because God knew that we all waver in our faith and need to know that we're not alone in our struggles.

For you, having your stuff together probably won't mean getting a house and land ready for your spouse. But if by "having your stuff together" we mean trusting that

God will walk with you through the unknowns, then we hope your answer is the same as Abraham's when he finally surrendered control in his life:

A big *yes* to God…whatever the journey ahead.[6]

But a word of wisdom as you travel. In order to *enjoy* the ride to the peak, it's a good idea to look at the different gauges we have talked about in this book. If a gauge in your life is on "*E*," then from experience, I highly recommend you pull over and take care of it.

It makes the ride much more enjoyable.

---

6   "In his heart a man plans his course, but the LORD determines his steps." (Proverbs 16:9)

∞ this is forever....do I really want this?

....

At the close of the wedding ceremony, as the couple stood before me (Byron), they poured colored sand together into one glass container as a symbol of their marital covenant and their joining of lives. Together T.J.'s brown sand and Jessica's blue sand formed a beautiful image of their marriage, the colors representing each person's uniqueness and the one jar representing their common life.

By faith, they were moving forward.

"By faith…"

So much happens in that one little phrase. A journey into the unseen, trusting that whatever lies ahead God will help us navigate through it all. It's impossible to see the future, so we can only take those steps…

…by faith.

We begin a relationship for all sorts of reasons, but as the relationship develops and God does what He's so good at doing with His people—working all things together for good[1]—we begin to ask the tough questions about the future. We ask others their opinions by our inquisitiveness. We weigh the pros and cons of the relationship by reason and careful thought. We watch the other person by close observation over time. We look to Scripture in trust. We pray out of gratitude

---

1   Romans 8:28

and need. And then there comes a time when the decision to marry—after all we know about the person—has to be by faith.

By faith….

Faith is not a blind leap, as some say. Jumping into marriage "trusting" that God will somehow patch together the fairytale answer we hope, in spite of the fact that we haven't wrestled with the tough questions, isn't faith—it's foolishness. Instead, faith is stepping in the direction we sense God leading us in—recognizing our own inability—trusting that He knows what lies around the corner and that he'll be there walking beside us *whatever* happens. That it probably won't all work out as we anticipate, but that He'll *make* it work out, working all things for good.

As you finish this book, perhaps you have a little more clarity regarding the future of your relationship. Like Rowdy and Anna, by faith you may decide to call it off. Or, like Kyle and Jen, by faith you may decide to move forward. Then again, right now you may be left with more questions than answers.

If so, you're in precisely the right place.

Because God isn't intimidated by your questions. He welcomes them. As you wrestle to "know that you know," it is through that very restlessness that those tough questions form. Intimate relationships shine a light deep into the inner cavern of our souls to expose who we are and what we truly believe.

And God invites us on a hunt with Him in search of answers to those questions.

"The Fundamental Fact of Existence…"

In the New Testament book of Hebrews, we read that "the fundamental fact of existence is that this trust in God, this faith, is the firm foundation under everything that makes life worth living. It's our handle on what we can't see. The act of faith is what distinguished our ancestors, set them above the crowd."[2]

2   Hebrews 11:1 (*The Message*)

Faith distinguished those heroes of the faith, though it's easy to forget all they went through to become people full of faith—*faith-ful.* Instead we focus on their faithful actions, not the struggle they went through: With cultural expectations. With doubt. With the sin that so easily entangled them. Yet in the end all were considered heroes of faith.

> *Therefore, since we are surrounded by such a great cloud of witnesses, let us throw off everything that hinders and the sin that so easily entangles, and let us run with perseverance the race marked out for us.*[3]

Any athlete will play better before a good crowd, and we are told that we are playing before the watchful eyes of the best crowd, those heroes of the faith: Abel, Moses, the Israelites, Enoch, Abraham, Rahab, and Noah. Each one of them know from experience the difficulties in living a life of faith, in trusting God. Each one of them can sympathize with the struggle you're engaged in right now.

Listen closely to their stories and those of others of those who have gone before you, who have walked into the unknown by faith. For just as each one of them stepped out in faith, trusting God's ways above their own…

> *By faith, Rowdy and Anna considered the pressures around them and reconsidered their marriage as they saw their paths diverging from the other.*

> *By faith, Kyle re-considered his expectations—tossed his "perfect" list, exchanging it for God's call on his life—and married Jen.*

> *And by faith, Carla and I acted on what we knew about each other—and what we each knew about God and His example of love—to step into marriage.*

---

3   Hebrews 12:1-2

Each person's story is different, but all touch on the themes of faith, hope, and love. So often we want life to be easy, but God wants our lives to be good—*very good*—so that we grow in spiritual maturity.

So let us fix our attention on Christ…whatever our own journey ahead.

Spilling Over.

As T.J. and Jessica poured out their colored sand, they began trying to outdo each other (both are extremely competitive), each pouring faster. But she beat him to it. She dumped out her entire jar, filling the container. Everyone laughed. But not about to stand there with sand remaining in his own jar, T.J. kept pouring until his sand spilled out over the lip of the container and down onto the table. He kept pouring and pouring until every last grain was on the table. Empty. Which, since God loves metaphors, is a great picture of how our love should be.

The first to pour ourself out.

The one to give to overflowing.

Demonstrating a deep love for each other.

A covenant love that comes from God.

As we love here and now…

…*before forever*.

Watch what God does, and then you do it, like children who learn proper behavior from their parents. Mostly what God does is love you. Keep company with him and learn a life of love. Observe how Christ loved us. His love was not cautious but extravagant. He didn't love in order to get something from us but to give everything of himself to us. Love like that.

-Ephesians 5:1-2 (*The Message*)

connect with _ God

index of driving questions

016 is it time to consider moving from commitment to covenant?

017 are our parents for or against it? does it really matter?

about Legacy Family Ministries

Our mission—Why we exist?

The reason this ministry exists is to pass on God's principles from one generation to another:

- By *deepening the roots of individuals* with God's truth through mentoring, teaching, speaking, and writing.
- By *developing the foundation of pre-engaged and engaged couples* to grow in Christ and make family a priority through curriculum instruction on relationships, mate selection, and marriage preparation.
- By *encouraging busy families* to focus on what is most important -- God and each other through church/community conferences, retreats, and parent forums.

Our vision—What we want to become?

Through fulfilling the purpose and vision our hope is to deepen the roots of individuals with God's truth so that their foundation as a married couple will be developed for the sake of the family institution. By strengthening the family they will in turn pass on God's principles from one generation to the next. Throughout Scriptures the idea of passing on a Biblical legacy is consistent. A society is influenced by the truth of God being taught to the next generation.

about our marriage preparation course

...it takes 3 for 2 to become one!

Countdown is a marriage preparation course for engaged couples consisting of eight sessions of Bible study, interaction, and practical teaching. Topics such as the purpose for marriage, roles and responsibilities, financial responsibilities, emotional responsibilities, spiritual responsibilities, sex, communication and conflict resolution, in-laws, and goal setting are discussed. This totals about 28+ hours of pre-marital preparation and counseling. We have two options: 1) seven-week class that concludes with a weekend retreat and 2) The Weekender – This is a condensed version of the seven-week course taking place during a weekend retreat.

Of the almost 1,000 couples who have gone through the course since 1995, less than 4% have ended in divorce. Our desire is to develop the foundation of engaged couples to grow in Christ and make family a priority.

Each week a couple is given 4 to 5 learning activities concerning the upcoming topic. The format will be something like meditating on a scripture passage, doing a Biblical word study, listening to an audio CD, going to a romantic place, anything that creatively challenges your thinking...etc. Nothing major or extremely time consuming, but vital to working through issues together and alone.

We want to hear from you.
Please send your comments about this book to us in care of:

Byron and Carla Weathersbee
Legacy Family Ministries
PO Box 20324
Waco, TX 76702-0324

(254)-772-0412 | office@legacyfamily.org | www.legacyfamily.org

notes

notes

about the authors:

Dr. Byron and Carla Weathersbee co-founded Legacy Family Ministries in 1995 to pass on Biblical principles from one generation to another by providing marriage preparation for pre-engaged and engaged couples. They have written and developed a marriage prep curriculum and Leaders' Guide— *Countdown…It Takes 3 for the 2 to Become One*, and produced an audio CD— *Countdown to Sexual Intimacy* for engaged couples.

The Weathersbees were married on June 16, 1984. They have three children, Bo, Brittney, and Casey. They both graduated from Baylor University. Carla has done graduate work at Baylor in Exercise Physiology. Byron earned an Ed. D. in Leadership from The Southern Baptist Theological Seminary and holds an M.A.R.E. from Southwestern Baptist Theological Seminary.

In addition to being a full time mom to three children, Carla provides leadership and direction to Legacy Family Ministries' marriage prep classes. She teaches a weekly Bible study at her church, and meets regularly with college women. Dr. B currently serves as Vice President for Student Life at the University of Mary Hardin-Baylor in Belton, Texas. In addition to serving on church staffs for 15 years, he served Baylor as the interim University Chaplain, Sports Chaplain, and a lecturer in Health, Human Performance, and Recreation. Back in 1995, the Weathersbees helped plant an innovative church, University Baptist Church in Waco, Texas, who ministers primarily to a new generation.

We want to hear from you.
Please send your comments about this book to us in care of:

Byron and Carla Weathersbee
Legacy Family Ministries
PO Box 20324
Waco, TX 76702-0324

(254)-772-0412 | office@legacyfamily.org | www.countdowntomarriage.com